SPIRITUAL
LIFE IN THE
CONGREGATION

A Guide for Retreats

SPIRITUAL LIFE IN THE CONGREGATION

A Guide for Retreats

RUEBEN P. JOB

UPPER ROOM BOOKS
NASHVILLE

The Upper Room Web site: www.upperroom.org

Scripture quotations not otherwise identified are from the New Revised Standard Version of the Bible, copyright 1989 by the Division of Christian Education of the National Council of the Churches of Christ in the USA and are used by permission.

Cover Design: Bruce Gore
Interior Design and Layout: Nancy Cole
First Printing: July 1997 (5)

Library of Congress Cataloging-in-Publication Data

Job, Rueben P.
    Spiritual life in the congregation : a guide for retreats / Rueben P. Job.
        p.   cm.
    Includes bibliographical references.
    ISBN 0-8358-0818-1
    1. Retreats—Christianity.   I. Title.
    BV5068.R4J64   1997   97-11425
    269'.6—dc21   CIP

Printed in the United States of America

For all who yearn to live with God

CONTENTS

Preface 9

Introduction 11

PART I: FOUNDATIONS FOR CONGREGATIONAL RETREATS

1. Some Distinctive Kinds of Spiritual Life Retreat 17
2. Biblical and Theological Foundations for Spiritual Retreats 21
3. Essential Elements of Spiritual Life Retreats 27
4. Preparing for Retreat 31
5. Planning for a Retreat 43

PART II: CONTINUING THE JOURNEY/NURTURING NEW LIFE

6. Opportunities and Dangers of Reentry 51
7. Facing the Head Winds 53
8. Conserving the Gift 57
9. Discovering, Developing, and Deploying Spiritual Leaders 63

PART III: RETREAT DESIGNS

Considerations When Designing a Retreat 67

Retreat Designs

Design #1: A Church-wide Retreat 71

Design #2: A Youth Retreat 77

Design #3: An Older Adult Retreat 87

Design #4: A Personally Guided Retreat 91

Design #5: A Private Retreat 103

Design #6: An Action Retreat 109

Creating and Using a Retreat Checklist 115

A Retreat Planning Checklist 117

Bibliography and Additional Resources 119

Prayers, Hymns, and Meditations for Persons on Retreat 121

Endnotes 128

PREFACE

I have received more than two hundred requests to design and lead retreats for a great variety of groups from every section of our country. In each case the retreat design was fashioned to fit the needs and setting of the retreat. The first one of these experiences was twenty-five years ago. I had so much to learn. The last one was a few weeks ago. I have so much to learn!

What follows in this guide is a compilation of what I have learned from others and from the experience of going apart to be with God with a great variety of groups. It also reflects the truths and insights that have come from the privilege of walking with many in personally guided retreats. This guide is a work in progress. It makes no attempt to be the last word. It does attempt to give simple and understandable guidance for the pastor and lay leader who seeks to strengthen the spiritual life of those in their care.

I am especially grateful to all those individuals and groups who have taught me to listen for, hear, and respond to the voice of God. My desire is that the following pages will effectively pass on what others have given to me.

A special word of gratitude to Upper Room Editors, George Donigian and George Knight, for their patience with me and their contribution to my work.

INTRODUCTION

For nearly two decades I have been privileged to lead retreats in nearly every part of our country. The retreats have always been designed for specific purposes and for each individual or community that was to participate. The settings ranged from noisy hotels to quiet retreat centers, and from inner city locations to rural countryside.

In each of these experiences there have been some common elements and themes that seem to have some universal application. Some of these themes and common elements of retreats will be found throughout this guide.

You have in your hand a resource that offers help for congregational leaders, lay and clergy, who are called upon to give spiritual leadership through a spiritual formation retreat. It has been created for pastors and other congregational leaders who desire to foster spiritual growth and vitality in the congregation. Using this guide as a resource, lay and clergy leaders will be able to design and conduct a retreat for almost every conceivable group in the congregation.

The second section of the guide is designed for retreat follow-up but will offer direction for every pastor and lay leader who desires a more faithful congregation and a setting in which personal faith may grow. Congregations are moving from activity for the sake of activity to activity designed to nurture the participant's relationship with God. This resource is a simple guide that can help any leader or group prepare for, design, plan, carry out, and follow up on an effective and successful retreat.

The suggestions and designs grow out of the experience gained from hundreds of retreats and from many retreat leaders. This resource is designed so that any leader, lay or clergy, with God's help, can lead effective retreats in the congregation.

There is great hunger for God today. Retreat houses are busy, and skilled retreat leaders have a dozen invitations to lead a retreat for every one they have time and energy to accept. Pastors and lay leaders are trying to give strong leadership in the area of spiritual formation. They desire to have those within their care experience the transforming power of a well-designed, well-planned, and well-carried-out retreat. Often the training and background for retreat leadership is not readily available. Consequently, it seemed wise to prepare a simple guide, accessible and usable by the experienced and the novice in retreat leadership.

Spiritual retreats have proven to be one of the significant ways of encounter with God. From Abraham and Moses to Jesus and now to us, the custom or spiritual discipline of withdrawing for a time of concentrated companionship with God has proven to be a transforming experience for individuals, congregations, and small groups. Retreats are a proven and effective way of opening our lives as individuals and as community to God's presence, guidance, healing, will, and way.

Retreats offer opportunity to listen for the voice of God in decision making and in our spiritual journey. They are uniquely effective in providing satisfying food for hearts that are hungry for God. Retreats are also a way of caring for the soul, nurturing and sustaining life in the spirit for young and old alike.

While we will spend much of this guide thinking about what we will do and how we will do it, the fact remains that spiritual retreat is not so much about what we will do or our initiative as it is our response to God's initiative in calling us to closer companionship. In spiritual retreat we do not have the first word. In retreat we are awakened to God's call to us. We respond to God's gracious invitation to be fully present to God as God promises to be fully present to us.

Furthermore, we do not have the last word in spiritual retreats. As we are sent into the world following retreat, we are assured that we are not alone but that the Holy Spirit travels with us to guide and sustain us throughout life.

The following pages give some theological foundation and some practical help in designing, planning, and conducting retreats in the congregation. From purpose and site selection to leadership preparation and follow-up, you will find an easy-to-use guide for the multiple actions required for a successful retreat.

In the third part of this volume you will find numerous retreat designs for use with a variety of groups and in a variety of settings. The second section of the guide provides suggestions on ways to incorporate the experience of the retreat into daily life, as well as some readily available resources to feed and nurture participants following the retreat.

Part I

Foundations for Congregational Retreats

1 Some Distinctive Kinds of Spiritual Life Retreat

Not all retreats are the same. It is nearly impossible to exhaust the great variety of retreat experiences that have roots in our biblical and theological heritage. We have so many different needs, find ourselves in so many different settings, and bring such a great variety of life experience and faith to each retreat experience that not every kind of retreat or retreat design will be an exact fit for us every time.

A brief review of some traditional types of retreats can help us to see the scope of retreat ministry and also help us decide the kinds of retreats appropriate for different groups.

At least four distinct kinds of retreats are frequently practiced: (1) dialogical, (2) personally guided, (3) preached, and (4) private. Each has similarities to the others and yet each has many distinctive qualities. Because this is true, it is important to be clear about focus and audience before deciding the kind of retreat that will be most helpful.

Many of us who are familiar with junior high and senior high camping of the last twenty years will have seen or perhaps experienced preached or taught retreats. A preached/taught retreat is common to many youth camp experiences and is centered around a speaker or leader who presents the content of the retreat in a teaching or preaching mode. Usually there is also time for reflection and small group interaction. This may be the most easily planned and conducted retreat. It is also an easy entrance into the retreat experience for the participant who has never had a retreat experience.

Dialogical retreats rely more heavily upon interaction of the participants and may be a natural next step for persons who have had some experience as participants or as leaders in a preached or taught retreat. Dialogue is the center around which the activities of this retreat revolve.

The design includes some input times by the leader and usually involves some specific questions to guide the discussion of the small groups.

If the content of the retreat is complex or controversial or if the participants are inexperienced in small group life, it may be necessary to have trained small group leaders to facilitate the process work in each of the groups. This need will surface as the retreat is being planned and steps can then be taken to train or provide small group facilitators.

2. Personally guided retreats are usually done with a small group under the guidance of one spiritual guide. The size of the group may vary but should usually not be more than nine persons. However, if experienced guides are provided for each group, the number can be much larger. This kind of retreat is more focused on each individual and involves relatively brief presentations by the leader, large blocks of time for personal reflection, and significant face-to-face time with the leader or spiritual guide.

The design for such a guided retreat includes large blocks of time for reflection, reading, prayer, and a great deal of silence. Silence is a wonderful gift of God but often seems threatening to the inexperienced participant. And yet, silence is important in helping us to create some space for God in our lives. To shut out the other voices and listen only for the voice of God is rarely done outside a retreat experience. Careful planning and utilization of silence is one of the most important things any planning team or leader can do.

For extroverts silence is as difficult as flying but for introverts it is as easy as falling. Introverts expend little energy or effort to enter into deep silence. Extroverts do expend a great deal of energy to enter into silence and will often spend a great deal of energy resisting silence. It is important for the retreat leader to recognize this distinction and be able to offer acceptance and encouragement to those who are having difficulty with silence.

3. Private retreats are often used by persons seeking discernment on personal matters, or where no spiritual guide is available. Some have suggested the importance of a private retreat every month for every leader in the church. (See *A Guide to Prayer* by Rueben P. Job and Norman Shawchuck and *A Guide to Retreat* by Rueben P. Job.)

There are many biblical examples of private retreat as individuals sought solitude to find God and God's way. Perhaps the most notable is the experience of Jesus for forty days in the wilderness.

Private retreats may be built around a scripture passage, a classic text in spirituality, or a contemporary spiritual reading resource. At other times the retreat will be formed around the need of the person and perhaps most frequently around the basic themes of the spiritual life.

There may be an intermingling of some of these characteristics in every retreat that is planned. The boundaries of these definitions are fluid and the definition itself is offered not as a rigid structure but only to assist you in the planning, preparation, and conducting of spiritual retreats in the congregation.

It is important to be aware of some of the options available as you plan a retreat. The type of retreat you choose will be determined by the purpose, setting, and participants of the retreat. Suggested designs for each type of retreat are offered in the third section of this guide.

2 BIBLICAL AND THEOLOGICAL FOUNDATIONS FOR SPIRITUAL RETREATS

While there is great interest in spirituality today, the term defies precise definition. There are a large number of definitions that can be used to describe what many people simply refer to as "our walk with God." The entire Bible is the story of humankind's walk with God. Sometimes that walk was faithful and rewarding and sometimes it was unfaithful and disastrous.

As Christians we are always on the "way to Emmaus" (see Luke 24:13-27), and there is One who travels with us even though this other One often goes unrecognized. This journey is our spiritual life.

We have been created for companionship with God. It is hard to believe, but true, that God desires to relate to us and to commune with us throughout all of life. But as in any healthy relationship, our relationship with God requires our participation. Spiritual retreats are one way in which we become aware of God's companionship with us and desire for our companionship as well.

The Bible is filled with stories and statements that speak directly to our walk with God and God's companionship with us. From the words of Jesus that promise the indwelling presence of God in John 14:23 to the comprehensive description of life in Christ in Ephesians 3:14-21, spirituality is seen more as the work of God within us than our work of seeking God.

The Gospel of John declares that God seeks to make our hearts home. The availability of the indwelling God to each of us is an important element in spiritual formation. Ultimately, our spiritual life is shaped and determined by the God who is at the center of our life.

Walter Brueggemann says that Christians have to do with a particular God—a God made known in Old and New Testaments, creation, centuries of experience with this God, and most fully made known in the life, death, and resurrection of Jesus Christ.[1] And it is this God who calls us to companionship in the whole of life. We fashion our response to this God on the basis of the God whom we worship and follow. We fashion our response to God according to the image of God that we constantly hold before us.

One of the reasons spirituality is so difficult to define is that spirituality has to do not only with our own souls but with God. And the Holy Spirit is not easily contained in any description or definition. It is equally difficult to control the Holy Spirit so we cannot predict where or how God will break into our lives, be made known to us, or respond in love to our awakened love for God. Therefore, no one structure of spirituality and no single definition can contain the reality.

Ephesians puts it this way, "Grant that you may be strengthened in your inner being with power through his Spirit, and that Christ may dwell in your hearts through faith, as you are being rooted and grounded in love" (Eph. 3:16-17).

Spirituality has to do with a God who makes God's self known. The creation, the events of history, the scriptures, the traditions of the faithful, our own daily lives—all of these are important bearers of God's self disclosure. But for the Christian the supreme voice of God is Jesus Christ. "In him the fullness of God was pleased to dwell" (Col. 1:19) is how the author of Colossians puts it.

Therefore, when we want to see God, hear God's voice, know God, share intimate communion with God, and live a lifetime of companionship with God, we turn to Jesus Christ, for in him we have the most complete revelation of the fullness of God.

Marjorie J. Thompson in her book *Soul Feast* declares, "Scripturally speaking, the spiritual life is simply the increasing vitality and sway of God's Spirit in us. It is a magnificent choreography of the Holy Spirit in the human spirit, moving us toward communion with both Creator and creation."[2]

Her words give witness to the vital and dynamic nature of spirituality. Therefore, our efforts to contain the whole of the spiritual life in stages of growth, or life maps, or seasons of the soul, or any other tightly structured model of spirituality is impossible but does lead to some important leanings.

1. **Structure cannot contain the Spirit of God.** Just when we think we have captured the Holy Spirit and channeled the power of the Spirit in a model, method, or a new paradigm, we discover once again that the Holy Spirit cannot be bound and God meets us and walks with us in ways that we do not always comprehend and almost always never expect.

2. **Spirituality has to do with the character of God** before it has to do with us, for spirituality, as life itself, is grounded in God, in the nature of God and in God's intention for humankind.

3. **Spirituality is where God's decisive action and our response meet.** It is this interaction with God rather than with structures, models, methods, or even experiences that defines spirituality. Structures, models, methods, and disciplines may position us to experience God's presence more fully, but they do not in and of themselves have the power to make God known to us. Only God can make God known to us. We can practice the disciplines and seek the models and structures that can open our lives to God's self-disclosure, but ultimately God alone can reveal God to us.

4. **Spirituality is a journey, not a destination.** As long as we live we will be on a spiritual journey because we are spiritual beings and our interaction with God will never plumb the depths of God's being. No matter who we are or where we are on our spiritual journey, we are just beginners because we have so much of our experience of God still ahead of us. Because God is infinite, our experience of God can never be exhausted and we will never arrive at the "end of our quest." This learning saves us from arrogance on the one hand and dismay on the other of comparing our "experience" or our "progress" to that of other persons.

Kenneth Leech has written a book, *Experiencing God: Theology as Spirituality*, in which he strives to answer the question, "Who is this God of Christian spirituality?" We may not be able to read Leech's book, but we can listen to our own tradition, confidently search the scriptures, turn to Jesus, read and reflect upon the written record of the saints, and finally trust the Holy Spirit for the answer to this question.

Jesus himself reminds us that we have to do with a covenant-making God. His last meal with the disciples was declared to be the new covenant. The covenant theme begins in Genesis with Adam and continues through Abraham and then Moses and David and finally comes to fulfillment in Jesus. Jesus was the utter trustworthiness and fidelity, and the unconditional love of God incarnate.

In looking at Jesus we begin to understand the love and fidelity of this covenant-making God. It is this God with whom we have to do in our spiritual life. "God is faithful; by him you were called into the fellowship of his Son, Jesus Christ our Lord" (1 Cor. 1:9).

This covenant-making and covenant-keeping God promises to be with us, to relate to us as beloved children, to companion us in this life and the life to come. No chaos or catastrophe can overcome this mighty God, and no power can snatch us from the presence and care of this covenant-making God.

God is faithful. God can be trusted. God is able to provide. God keeps promises. God is tender and compassionate as well as mighty and just. God invites all to come home and live all of life in intimate relationship with God. God is love. This is the picture that Jesus gives us of God.

Christian spirituality is initiated and fulfilled by this covenant-making God. We are invited to respond, and spiritual retreats are an excellent way for us to pay attention to this covenant-making God in more focused ways. Spiritual retreats also give us wonderful opportunity to respond to God, establishing or renewing our own covenant with God.

If our spiritual lives are like the Emmaus walk, retreat is like the meal when Jesus was recognized in the breaking of bread. Food for the journey is always available but often appropriated and appreciated more fully during a spiritual life retreat.

While retreats are often held at some location other than a church building, congregational life is the ideal home for a retreat ministry. There is no other more ready community than congregation to listen intently for the voice of God, seek seriously for God's way, and faithfully respond to God's awakening call.

Congregational life is intended to be the fertile soil in which spiritual life is born, blossoms, and bears fruit. Congregational life is the best place to support individuals and families in their spiritual journey. Congregational life is where people learn what it means to follow Christ and to live the Christian life. Congregational life is where love for God, love for self, and love for neighbor can be learned, practiced, and incorporated into daily living.

Retreat ministry is one very important and effective way of supporting this central purpose of the congregation. Many times the retreat experience provides the opportunity for unusual growth in discipleship and almost unparalleled occasion for the nurture of the spiritual life of participants. Retreat is an opportunity for every congregation to provide unique and effective care for the soul of each member from youth to older adults.

Thomas Merton is supposed to have said that Americans feel guilty every time they slow down. Retreat gives a congregation a chance to slow down and simply to be with God. Retreat may not be essential for everyone, but it is certainly a proven method for those who want to know God more fully and to walk with God more faithfully in all of life.

The experience of going apart to be with God is as old as our record of God's people in the Bible. From Genesis to Revelation, going apart to be with God is encouraged, affirmed, and modeled. Witness the experience of Jacob at Bethel (Gen. 28:10-22), Moses on Mount Sinai (Exod. 19), the transfiguration of Jesus in the company of Peter, James, and John (Matt. 17:1-13), and the many times Jesus withdrew alone or with the disciples to pray and rest.

It is foolish and arrogant to assume that we can walk with God and live as faithful disciples without times of going apart, ascending the mountain, or casting our nets into the deep. If such going apart—

retreat—was a necessity for the giants of the faith, how much more important it is for us who desire to live with God in the world.

Spiritual life can be and should be nurtured in every contact with the congregation. The building, worship, meetings, fellowship, teaching, hospitality, communication, leadership, and every aspect of congregational life should be providing opportunity for new birth, nurture, and growth in our spiritual lives.

Even when each element of congregational life provides optimum opportunity for spiritual growth, retreat is still a necessary and effective part of a comprehensive ministry to the spiritual life of individuals, groups, families, and the entire congregation.

Retreat has great potential in helping persons experience heightened awareness and growth in life's most crucial relationship—our relationship to God. And this experience invariably results in a greater awareness and growth in relationship to others. Jesus' own going apart not only affirmed and strengthened his relationship with God but also prepared him and energized him for his relationship with and ministry to others.

Retreat experiences lead to engagement experiences. Those who have been close to God in retreat begin to think like God and even their actions become Godlike, and this inevitably leads them to the action cycle of Christian spirituality.

God's people have always experienced their faithful relationship with God as journey. Just as Moses led the people toward the Promised Land, we too are bound for the promised land of closer and even unbroken relationship with God—relationship that results in greater trust, confidence, joy, service, and ultimately full realization of God's unconditional love and abiding presence.

Retreat experiences are a valuable method which congregations can use to help each member and the larger community in their journey toward God.

3 ESSENTIAL ELEMENTS OF SPIRITUAL LIFE RETREATS

There is potential for great variety in the content and conduct of a spiritual life retreat. However, in a Christian spiritual life retreat there are some essential elements that do bring common shape and structure to them all. These elements are simple but essential to the success and faithfulness of the retreat.

These elements will be discussed at more depth at various places throughout our guide as we think about their specific application to our preparation, planning, conducting, and follow-up responsibilities. This brief listing is intended to help us in our overall planning for Christian retreat.

Jesus Christ is the cornerstone and sacred scripture is at the very heart of Christian retreat. To be Christ-centered is to measure every aspect of the retreat against the standard of Jesus. To be Christ-centered is to keep the focus on Jesus and not upon any other person or any other theology. To be Christ-centered is to remember that retreat design and retreat leadership's prime responsibility is to reflect the light of Christ.

Having Christ as the center means that we will naturally draw heavily from the Bible. When in the course of planning a retreat, we may consider a passage of scripture as the basis for the retreat. Or, we may consider a theme and use a number of passages to bring light and insight to the subject. This works especially well in a discernment retreat but can be a helpful method for every retreat experience.

While other sacred reading may not rank next in importance, it is important to consider how the participants can benefit from the experience of the saints who have gone before us. Some retreat designs call for reading a common spiritual classic in preparation for the retreat. Other designs draw heavily from a wide variety of those who have journeyed with Christ through the centuries that preceded our walk with God today. Still other designs are shaped around a common theme and draw upon the insights of a particular leader in the field.

An ancient illustration would be an Ignatian model of discernment and a contemporary one, ways of prayer as suggested by Richard Foster in *Prayer: Finding the Heart's True Home* or spiritual nurture as outlined in *Soul Feast* by Marjorie J. Thompson.

Prayer is another foundational element of Christian retreat. In Richard J. Foster's book, *Prayer: Finding the Heart's True Home*, he discusses at length twenty-one kinds of prayer. We may be unfamiliar with some of the types of prayer that Foster mentions, but we cannot imagine a Christian retreat without a generous amount of time given to various methods and forms of prayer.

Opportunities to learn how to pray from others are very rare. Most of us learn to pray by accident rather than by intention. Spiritual retreat can expand our understanding and experience of Christian prayer.

Time and our utilization of time are essential elements in every retreat experience. A significant block of time is required for any retreat. How this time is used becomes a key factor in the helpfulness of the retreat.

Space is as ordinary as time but critical to the retreat experience. Almost any space can become sacred space for the participants. But it is true that some space lends itself to becoming sacred space more readily than others. The importance of the selection and preparation of sacred space cannot be overemphasized.

Silence was mentioned earlier in this guide, but it bears further attention. It is one of the most neglected gifts given for spiritual growth. Sometimes it is said that introverts long for silence and solitude, and extroverts flee silence and solitude. However, it is true that all personality types can appropriate the gift of silence in wonderful and transforming ways. The retreat design and the retreat leader can ensure that this gift is used effectively.

Shared life story should be one part of our congregational life. But often it is neglected in congregational life and in retreat. The design team and retreat leader will want to secure the necessary time and create the hospitable environment for honest sharing of life story. The leadership should make certain that the retreat is a safe place to be honest.

It will be necessary, early in the retreat, to declare the importance of confidentiality, acceptance, and openness to each other. Trust can only grow in an environment where confidences are kept, where acceptance is without reservation, and where every person is seen as a beloved sister or brother.

The sharing of our life stories in a retreat experience can be a forerunner to a more open interaction within the entire life of the congregation. Since we are each a part of God's grand design of creation, we each have a contribution to make in proclaiming God's story. In other words, God's story, the proclamation of the Good News, cannot be complete until each of us shares our part of that great story of love and redemption. The retreat designs should include a variety of methods to facilitate this part of the retreat experience.

You will note some suggestions in the retreat designs that appear in the third section of this guide. You note that questions are often used to help persons respond in safe areas and safe ways. As trust grows, deeper questions and depth of sharing become possible.

Every retreat should have a variety of methods to cultivate interaction among the participants. Such simple things as seating arrangements should be considered, as well as plenary, small group, dyad, and triad discussions. Worship, fellowship, meals, break times, and recreation provide still other opportunities to assist participants to interact, listen to, and learn from one another's experience.

4 PREPARING FOR RETREAT

There is no fixed formula for our journey toward God, and there is no single model for retreat. The third section of this guide suggests a number of retreat designs that you may use as they are or adapt to your particular need. But first I invite you to carefully consider the first step in any successful retreat—preparation.

Many people suggest that planning a retreat is the first step. You may come to that conclusion as you consider a retreat experience for your congregation. And yet, it seems that preparation is more central to the life of the retreat than is planning. The success of any retreat is often determined weeks and months in advance as persons begin to pray and listen to the voice of God in scripture, their own life experience, the events going on around them, and the experience of those who will participate in the retreat.

Preparation can help individuals and the entire congregation identify their own yearning for God and can help them to seek ways in which to address this yearning.

It is well for the pastor, or whoever is responsible for the retreat, to consider naming a small task group on preparation. This task group will create anticipation, expectancy, and readiness on the part of the entire congregation. The material in the following pages are intended to give some guidance to the preparation task group.

PREPARATION OF THE LEADER

Preparation of the leader or leadership team is one of the major elements of a successful retreat ministry. In many ways the retreat leader is the content, the book that will be read first and remembered longest by the participants. This is one reason that preparation of the leadership of any retreat must be taken seriously and addressed early in the preparation for any retreat.

Mahatma Gandhi is said to have commented that the aroma of Christianity is more subtle than that of the rose. Francis de Sales suggested that the rose shouts its message to us even though the rose is silent. The rose is truly itself and does not need to prove itself to anyone. It simply *is* in all of its beauty and fragrance. Its integrity and fidelity are made known to all the senses.

Retreat leaders can best serve as channels for God's grace when they are truly themselves. There is no need to be someone else, but fully ourselves. Just like the rose, the fragrance and beauty of a retreat leader's life will linger long after the retreat has ended. This thought would be unbearable if we did not remember that we are not in this alone. We are in fact only the second person in a leadership role.

When we remember that the real leader is the Holy Spirit, our confidence returns and we can more easily accept the role that is ours as one of those called to retreat leadership. When we remember who the real leader is, our fears subside and we recognize that our "authority" as a retreat leader does not come from degrees but rather from a daily walk with God that is observed to be authentic and is reflected in everything we do.

Gwen White, whose gifts in retreat leadership have taken her to nearly every part of the country and every kind of retreat experience imaginable, says that the most precious asset we have as retreat leaders is our "authentic imperfect self." To be open, honest, and vulnerable is to encourage others to risk a closer and deeper look at their own walk with God.

Preparation of the leader is a lifelong process and is never fully completed. Ideally, we will continue to grow in our relationship to God as long as we live. If we do, we will be in a constant mode of preparation for retreat leadership. As we learn to walk with God in our own lives, we are given wisdom and grace to serve as guides to others as they seek to walk with God. As fidelity to God is incorporated into our daily walk, we become more and more able to represent God, and Christ can be seen in us. Spiritual growth is contagious and is caught more easily than taught.

It has long been known that we take on the qualities of those we are with and especially those we respect, love, or admire. Spouses and elderly sisters or brothers who have lived together a lifetime begin to think alike, act alike, and even look alike. So it is in our companionship with God. Living with God is a transforming and forming experience. Our own walk with God, even though faulty and stumbling, is our best preparation for retreat leadership.

Paying attention to our own journey with God is the best kind of preparation we can make. Establishing a way of living that is nurturing to our own spiritual life is a major step in our preparation to lead a spiritual life retreat. While it is important not to become too rigid, it is also important to establish some minimum disciplines. What is it that you do every day, every week, every month, every year to keep yourself in healthy and growing relationship with God?

While a more complete answer to this question is the content of another book, it is important to suggest that each day should be marked with some time for prayer and reflection on the scriptures and on daily life as a window to God. Corporate worship, Sabbath time, and some act of mercy and compassion may be suggestive for shaping your own way of living. A time apart for the leader or leadership team is also an important element in our own spiritual growth and in our preparation to lead others in their quest for God.

If we believe that the Holy Spirit is the true leader of retreat, then we will want to develop our own sensitivity to the Spirit's leadership so we can cooperate with the transforming work going on in the life of each participant. As we learn to trust God and to be responsive to God's call and presence in our lives and in the world, we will discover growing confidence in God's desire and ability to use our lives to draw others close to God.

As we experience God's transforming power within and see God's shaping of our lives, we will find it easier to believe that every life can be transformed by the power and presence of God in their lives.

Finally, it needs to be said clearly that spiritual retreat leaders are not perfect! There will be times when the pain of our questions will nearly overshadow our assurance of God's truth and presence. At other times we will be reminded of our own desperate need of God's gifts of grace. When these times occur, we will be tempted to think of ourselves as hypocrites and pretenders. And if we proclaim our own perfection, we will be just that.

However, if we honestly recognize our need and our weakness and also remember God's grace, we will be led to rely more fully on God and give witness to this dependence. Our imperfections and even our weakness can be used if offered honestly to God. The authentic self is the greatest gift we have to bring. We are, as Henri Nouwen says, "wounded healers." We have not arrived, but we are on a journey toward God.

Remembering who we are as children of God and remembering who God is can help us through those times when our own imperfections seem to be so formidable. The memory of the Tender Shepherd's love and care and the mighty Savior's power to redeem may serve to bring light to the shadow of imperfection that touches us all.

The God who calls you to this leadership will provide the wisdom, strength, and love that you need. Prepare yourself as well as you can and then put your trust in God. Do your best to be faithful and enjoy the opportunity of growth that the retreat presents.

When the doubts come and the imperfections seem too much, give thanks to God, for each of them is a reminder of your need of God and of God's grace. The following story illustrates the point very well.

> Once upon a time a certain rabbi lived in a mountain village near the border of Slovakia. He prayed and taught and listened to the people of the village. One day a distressed couple came to the rabbi. They needed his prayers. They wanted the blessing of a child and had been married long years without a child. They felt certain the prayers of this rabbi could shake the foundations of heaven. The rabbi answered that he would pray for them, but first he wanted to tell a story. In joy the couple listened.
>
> Three Hasidim long desired to spend the High Holy Days with the great rabbi, Reb Yaakov-Yitzhak of Lublin. Blind in one eye, this rabbi was renowned for his insights into the Talmud and Kabbala. Some said his vision went from earth to heaven and back. Pilgrims came from far and near to learn from this rabbi.

So the three Hasidim began walking to Lublin in Poland. They went without money and food on a journey of faith. They became weakened. Said one of the three, "It is no blessing that we should die of starvation on our way to see the rabbi. The Torah says that anything may be done to save a life. Let's do something."

One of the three suggested that one of them should be disguised as a rabbi. In this way, when they came to a village, the people would offer them hospitality. They would be fed and given shelter. None of the Hasidim wanted to use this deceit, but they knew they would not survive without food. They drew lots. One became disguised as a rabbi. Another became his assistant. The third man continued the journey as a Hasidim from the rabbi's village.

At the next village the people welcomed them. The disguised Hasidim were taken to the inn. The innkeeper offered them a place to ease their burdens and gave them food and drink. Then the innkeeper said to the one disguised as a rabbi, "Pray for my son. He is dying. The doctors offer no hope. But the prayers of a rabbi will enter the ears of the Most Holy One, blessed be he. Perhaps it is for this time that you have come."

The pseudo-rabbi looked at his friends for advice. They motioned to him to go with the innkeeper. Once in the game, they knew they could not stop their pretense. The pseudo-rabbi walked off with the innkeeper.

The next day the three Hasidim began to walk, but the innkeeper loaned them a carriage and a pair or horses to take them to Lublin. They spent Rosh Hashanah in Lublin and they studied under Rabbi Yaakov-Yitzhak. After Yom Kippur came the time to go home, but first they needed to return the carriage and horses. They drove to the village and the pseudo-rabbi began to feel fear. When he saw the innkeeper running at the carriage and shaking his arms, terror struck the pseudo-rabbi.

The innkeeper hugged the pseudo-rabbi. "Thank you, thank you, thank you. Your prayers have been answered. After you left, my son got up and began playing and working. The doctors shake their heads and do not understand why he lives. But it is because your prayers were heard."

The other two Hasidim became very puzzled. Was their friend really a rabbi? Did they misunderstand?

The pseudo-rabbi explained that he had stood silently by the boy's bed. Then he thought, "Most High One, this boy and his father need not be punished because I have fooled them. They think I'm a rabbi. I'm not. You know that I am a pretender. When I leave, this boy will die and his father will think that all rabbis are powerless. So not because of my prayers or my life, but because this innkeeper believes—what can it hurt to cure this boy?"

Then the rabbi looked at the couple who wanted a child and said that he would pray. "Most High One, this man and woman need not be punished because they think I am a powerful rabbi. I am nothing. I am a pretender, as we all are pretenders. So not because of my prayers, but because of this couple— what can it hurt to give them a child?"

A year later the man and woman brought their eight-day-old son for circumcision.

Indeed, no one is perfect. Not one of us perfectly reflects the presence of God. But the good news is that God takes as much of our life as we are willing to offer and transforms it into something good and beautiful.

The formation of spiritual leaders is always a process, not a completed work. While we are incomplete, we are on the journey toward wholeness. God is the One who transforms us, guides us, sustains us, uses even our imperfections, will see us through our darkness, and will finally see us safely home and into the light and love of God's presence.

PREPARATION OF THE CONGREGATION

Preparation of the congregation is also an important step toward a successful retreat. Everything that can be done to foster openness, honesty, trust, attentiveness, and receptivity to God will help to prepare members of the congregation for a retreat experience. Regular prayer, worship, study, service, witness, and practicing hospitality and fellowship are essential elements in this preparation.

Give opportunity for members, young and old alike, to tell their own stories in a safe setting and then to reflect upon the meaning of their story. This can foster openness to the work of the Spirit in their lives. Another person's story can also be a tremendous source of insight into our own life story.

As we get to know one another at some depth, our appreciation for each other grows and we find encouragement to move toward reconciliation and a closer community. We often get new and helpful glimpses of the story of God as we hear the story of a sister or brother.

Practicing hospitality is another important step in preparation for retreat and Christian discipleship. Creating a climate of invitation, warm support, welcome, and nurture is one of the most important tasks that any congregation can undertake. But often it is overlooked for more "pressing" matters such as finance, personnel, and facilities. The hospitality of a congregation is the first and most lasting impression that anyone is likely to have of the life of a congregation.

Congregational leaders will want to ask how easy it is for persons to enter into the life of the congregation and its various units. Questions like the following are worthy of serious reflection.

- What kind of welcome do new children receive in the church school?
- How are young people assimilated into the youth program of the church?
- How easy are adults brought into the life of the church?
- Is the congregation accepting and affirming of a great variety of social, educational, and financial levels within its membership?

- What is the climate and attitude of each church school class, every meeting?
- Does every visitor feel wanted, safe, and accepted?

It is not only important to see every visitor as Christ but to be able to see every member as Christ bearer.

Simple things like ample parking, clear signs, and directions to get to the church and to find particular things in the building, well-trained greeters and teachers who reflect the light and love of God in every contact with their class—these are some of the ways in which a congregation can extend Christian hospitality and help persons feel welcome and wanted.

It is this kind of environment that can prepare persons for retreat. In such a hospitable congregation, even casual observation of those around us will turn our thoughts and lives toward God and God's desire for all creation. This is the ultimate goal of each congregation and each retreat.

If the level of comfort for those visiting the congregation is high, they will likely be nurtured and will most often return. If the welcome is cool, overbearing, demanding, or threatening, it will be hard for visitors to sense God's presence and respond to God's call. It requires sensitivity and patience on the part of pastors and lay leaders to develop a leadership team and a congregation that consistently practices a high level of hospitality. But there are few things more important for the health and faithfulness of the congregation as well as spiritual retreat.

Creating the environment that invites the Spirit's presence, honors every person's unique gifts, and encourages faithful and consistent response to God will permit the transforming work of God to take place in the lives of individuals, families, and the entire congregation.

PREPARING THE SETTING FOR RETREAT

Once you have decided on the purpose and location of the retreat, you can give attention to preparing the setting. Sometimes it will be possible to have the use of a conference-style retreat center, another time a rustic camp setting, and at other times the church building will be the facility chosen.

While a retreat center is usually designed with retreats in mind, church buildings and even hotels and other public meeting space can be utilized for effective retreats.

A classroom in the church building will require different preparation than the fellowship hall of a church building or a motel. Each will require different preparation than a well-designed retreat center. Seating arrangements that permit persons to see one another, see and hear the leader, and interact with one another will be a primary consideration in preparing for the retreat.

Look at each space with the following questions in mind.

- Will this space make everyone feel at home?
- How will this space make people feel comfortable and at ease?
- How can this space be a window to God, helping us to see, know, and relate to God?
- How will this space encourage us to listen for and respond to the voice of God?
- How does this space make persons aware of God's presence?
- How can we make this space hospitable to God's present and the participants' presence?

These questions can help us see some of the barriers that may be linked with every retreat setting. Every setting has some disadvantages, and not all of them can be overcome. But to be aware of them will enable you to plan in a way that will limit their negative impact on the retreat. This exercise will also make you more aware of the strengths of the setting and how these strengths can be used to enhance the value of the retreat.

Simple steps can be taken to ensure that meeting rooms are carefully arranged with faith symbols such as flame, Bible, or cross that draw attention to God. Giving a committee or an individual responsibility for worship centers is sometimes the best way to ensure that space is worshipful for every part of the retreat.

If the facility is in an urban setting, it will be especially important to consider having flowers and living plants present. If the setting is rural, consider ways to incorporate part of the natural setting into the holy place of retreat. The purpose of this preparation is to bring awareness of God's presence to each participant.

Make certain that sleeping rooms are clean and comfortable and that meals are healthful as well as satisfying. Some persons who are on their first retreat may be anxious and tend to overeat. That is why it is important to have refreshing and healthful snacks and drinks for break times and for scheduled community or fellowship times.

It is also important to have small group space preselected and set up for the size of group that will be using it. Arrange the room so all participants can see each other as they speak. Chairs in a circle or around a table make it easier for each person to participate.

You will also want to check out recreation options for individuals and groups. Play is an important element in most successful retreats of twenty-four hours or more. To prepare for recreation ahead of time will ensure that it is seen as a part of the retreat rather than as something added on and "less spiritual." Keep the participants in mind when planning recreation. Older adults and young children generally have different requirements!

Preparing the setting should also include provision for an orderly, inviting, and nurturing registration process. An information packet that gives schedule, room assignments, and supportive material for the retreat should be available at the time of registration.

Have room assignments made ahead of time so each small group is designated at the time of registration through a system of numbers or letters on a name tag (this works well for homogeneous groups). If heterogeneous groups are desired, another system should be used to select persons for the small-group part of the retreat.

If you are planning an overnight retreat, have several persons available just to show participants to their rooms when they arrive and to answer any questions.

Not all of the setting preparations mentioned above are necessary for every facility. And there will be some instances when additional or a different kind of preparation will be required for an effective retreat.

However, the suggestions above can get you started on preparing a setting that enhances a positive retreat experience.

Imagine yourself in the setting. Then go over the retreat design and consider how each part of the schedule will be experienced by the participants. This practice tends to reveal what else can be done to prepare the setting for an optimum retreat experience.

5 PLANNING FOR A RETREAT

Preparing for a retreat and planning a retreat are two distinct functions. Preparing for a retreat involves readiness on the part of leader, participants, congregation, and setting. Planning has to do with the more practical aspects of the retreat itself, such as daily schedule, theme, time frame, and costs. Planning leads naturally into creating the design for the retreat you are planning. It is well to remember to ask questions like these:

- Why are we doing this?
- What is our purpose in planning this retreat?
- Who are the participants?
- Where will the retreat be held?
- What is the theme?
- What do we want to happen?

Some of these and other questions will be found in the master checklist for planning a retreat on page 117. Following the checklist is one way to remind the planning committee what needs to be done and when the task needs to be completed. You will find the master checklist a helpful tool, although you should feel free to adapt it to suit your own needs.

The first step will be to gather a small committee to help in planning the retreat. This committee will normally be chosen from among the persons for whom the retreat is planned. If the retreat is for the Sunday school, youth group, older adults, men, women, or governing or administrative board of the congregation, select persons from this group to form the planning committee.

This committee can provide helpful insight and resource to the leader. It is also an excellent time for the retreat leader to provide experience and training for future retreat leaders. Pay attention to those who seem to emerge as the leaders. Consider how they might be prepared to provide spiritual leadership in the congregation as well as to lead future retreats.

By the time a committee is named, the purpose, place, and participants have often been determined. If that is the case, the committee will want to review those decisions. If these decisions have not yet been made, they should be part of the committee's work.

Determining the purpose of the retreat is an important element in the journey toward a successful retreat.

- Is it to build community?
- Is it to deepen faith?
- Is it to discern God's will?
- Is it to turn participants more fully toward God?
- Is it to help participants experience a variety of ways of prayer?
- Is it to be a time of reconciliation and healing?
- Is it to be primarily a time set in the midst or around another event, such as a planning retreat?

You can see that each of these purposes will impact the planning that is done for the retreat. It is important to know the purpose of the retreat before planning goes very far.

To be clear about participants is also an important element in planning. Plans for schedule, content, leadership, and facilities will be greatly influenced by those who are expected to be participants in the retreat.

The next step is to create a calendar or time schedule for the retreat experience. When will the retreat be held and for how long? To plan a congregational retreat in less than six months will put some strain on leadership and the busy schedules of participants. How much time is needed for the retreat and how much time is actually available will determine the outside parameters of the schedule.

There is room for flexibility in retreat scheduling and the amount of time required. Many retreat planners have discovered that at least one overnight is necessary for a formative retreat experience. Two overnights are even better. However, a six-hour block of time, using a well-designed model, can also provide a very fruitful retreat experience.

Plan well in advance. Planning that is hurried is counterproductive. And late announcement about the retreat is certain to prevent some people from participating. Select a preferred date and announce the date at once so persons can place the event on their calendars.

Invite the congregation to be in prayer for the retreat, retreat leaders, and those who will participate. Develop an expectancy for and openness to God's intervention in the life of the retreat participants and the entire congregation. Expect the transforming power of God to be at work in the lives of those who will attend.

Begin planning how the energy, insight, and commitment gained at the retreat can be sustained and invested in the whole church and in the community. Find ways to legitimize the spiritual growth that has taken place. Give opportunity for testimony and witness about what happened in the lives of individuals and in the community while on retreat. The second section of this guide gives some specific suggestions about follow-up.

Once the date for the retreat has been selected, it is time to work on a daily schedule. What will a normal day look like at this retreat? Or, what will the six hours look like for a shorter retreat? It is important to know the major blocks of time that will be available. Many begin planning a retreat with just the three normal divisions of the day: morning, afternoon, and evening. The final creation of the daily schedule can come later as the retreat design is finalized.

Determine when the retreat will begin and at least tentative times for meals, breaks, and concluding worship times each evening, if the retreat involves an overnight.

The processes used in the retreat should be designed to invite everyone to full participation. It is well to have some processes that involve just two or three people. It is difficult for some people to contribute even in a small group. It is easier for many persons to share with just one or two others than to do so in a small group or a large plenary session.

Small group and plenary discussion time should be included in the planning. This will involve securing space and leadership for small groups and designing the processes that will be used with each. The retreat designs include some suggested processes to use, but feel free to adapt these to your individual situation.

A well-designed retreat will also have questions for reflection relating to the scriptures or themes being used. You will find examples in the retreat designs in the third section of this guide. The questions should be designed to help the participants look inward at their own spiritual life in all of its complexity and wonder. Beginning questions are designed so all can answer and so even the most timid person will be able to respond.

Every retreat should be framed and supported by worship and prayer. Begin and end each day with corporate worship. Sometimes morning, midday, and evening prayers can be incorporated into the schedule with ease. Corporate worship and prayer do not take the place of individual worship and prayer, but they are an important element in retreat experiences.

These corporate worship experiences help us realize that when we pray we are always in the company of others. Our growth experiences may have some private elements, but they are always set in the context of community. We do not grow best in isolation. We need the support, example, encouragement, direction, and inspiration that come from community. This is especially true in our worship experiences.

Music is a very formative experience for nearly every person. Select some well-known hymns for their ease of singing and for their familiar and important content. Select some new and less-familiar hymns that speak to the retreat design or the issues that influence the participants. Teach some new songs and some simple choruses that participants can remember and use to nurture their souls once the retreat has ended.

Leading music has never been a strength of mine, so I find it desirable to ask for help. If you as a retreat leader are unable to lead music, consider asking someone to help you.

We often make the mistake of trying to do too much in a retreat. We bring such a large agenda to most retreats that we are often kept from the very companionship with God that we desire. Try to keep the agenda simple and the schedule open and flexible. It is tempting to have every hour and every moment filled with activities. To do so is a big mistake and will limit the usefulness of the retreat experience.

Training events, conferences, and seminars are often designed to be filled with activity every moment. Retreats are designed to avoid the sense of busyness and activity. There must be time for reflection and contemplation. We all need time to listen quietly for the voice of God in scripture, our surroundings, and the events of our lives. Such time will not be available if every moment is filled with activity.

Because of our emphasis on activity, it will be difficult to convince some people that anything can happen unless we are "doing" something and every moment is filled with some planned activity. Since Jesus withdrew for prayer and reflection, it seems strange that we should think we do not need these quiet times.

Space in the daily schedule for silence, solitude, and reflection are absolutely essential. We live in such a noisy world and are often made anxious by silence because it is so rare and we are so unfamiliar with it. And yet silence may be the single most formative part of any retreat experience. Our words, our best processes are all incomplete and ineffective without the generous use of silence and solitude in our retreat plans.

Silence is one of God's greatest gifts. To help participants appropriate the gift of silence will in itself make the retreat worthwhile. Silence is necessary for listening. We cannot hear what God is saying to us if we are always speaking to others or someone else is always speaking to us. It will take intentional effort on the part of those designing the retreat and the retreat leaders to control the many voices so we can hear the One Voice necessary for our lives.

Believing that the Holy Spirit is the leader of the retreat and that each participant is fully capable of hearing and responding to God's call, it is important to design the retreat so it will allow time and space for personal reflection and prayer. In-depth thinking and praying is generally not possible in a few minutes or in space filled with noisy distractions.

Conversation, colleagues, and community are all important. But our part of spiritual growth and transformation can be done best in an environment that encourages encounter with God—an environment that is hospitable to the holy and invites God's presence and the participants' awareness of this presence. Such an environment will include generous blocks of time for silence and personal reflection.

I would never create a retreat design or lead a retreat without a generous application of silence. There is a time for talking and fellowship, but there is also a time for silence and personal reflection. Evelyn Underhill, in her book *In the Ways of the Spirit*, says that silence permits us to "be quiet with the voice of the One who has everything to tell us and nothing to learn from us."[3]

Be open and flexible as you plan your retreat. Listen for the prompting of the Holy Spirit and seek to obey what you hear. Remember that God loves the church and each retreat participant and desires to make the retreat experience a wonderful time of new discovery, spiritual growth, and companionship with God and God's people. Flexibility, openness, and a stance of listening are important in planning and in conducting a retreat.

Your own personal life of prayer and listening will help you in the planning and will prepare you to meet the unexpected that always occurs in every retreat. Begin focused prayer on the retreat preparation, planning, and retreat itself, and the follow-up. Make certain that persons participating in the regular worship services are encouraged to begin praying for the retreat.

Most of our lives are busy and demanding, and we often come to a retreat near the point of exhaustion. A well-constructed design that includes an overnight experience should include time for adequate rest. Further, the retreat leader will want to be sensitive to the needs of individuals in the retreat and give permission for rest to those who may need it during the day.

Part II

Continuing the Journey/ Nurturing New Life

6 OPPORTUNITIES AND DANGERS OF REENTRY

Reentry into daily routine after a retreat of any kind can be difficult. So much within us has changed while we were on retreat; perhaps we approach all of life from a different perspective. But change is not limited to those who have been on retreat. So much around us has changed while we were spending concentrated time apart with God. So much awaits our return, from delayed work to family demands.

You will discover that as a pastor or lay person giving leadership in retreat to a group from the congregation does not exempt you from the frustration of reentry. You have gained new insights and new relationships have developed as together you experienced God's transforming presence while on retreat. To incorporate those new insights into daily life and to be fair to those new relationships while picking up the tasks and routines you left behind will require intentional effort.

To ignore these changes that await you is to experience frustration and the risk of losing the new life that was nurtured while on retreat. The following pages are intended to help you to prepare for and experience a positive reentry into the life you left behind for a brief time. This is true for all of us and the pastor and lay leadership must be particularly sensitive to the experience of those returning from retreat, even if they are among the ones returning!

There is risk that retreat leadership and those on retreat can form an exclusive bond that shuts others out or turns them off. Remember the importance of inclusiveness and open yourself and the retreat community to others with the goal of making everyone feel like an "insider."

The greater risk is that those returning from retreat will be left on their own with no efforts to confirm the commitments made and nurture the growth that has developed. Guide those returning from retreat to existing programs and groups that will nurture the hunger for God that led them to a retreat experience in the first place.

If programs and groups to serve this role are not present, consider starting them. A quest group, a new Bible study group, even a retreat group can be an option. This is also an excellent time for the pastor and lay leadership to provide regular learning and growth opportunities focused on those who have experienced retreat but which are open to everyone.

The experience of others suggests that it is very easy to lose the new insight, the heightened awareness of God, and the new life that you and others have experienced while on retreat. The suggestions that follow can get you in touch with methods that you can use to stay present to God and God's sustaining grace and to help those in your care to do the same.

As Christians we believe that God is always present to us. We agree with the psalmist that it is impossible to escape God's presence (see Ps. 139:7-12). And yet we can drift away from awareness of that Presence and forget that there is One who companions us in life's journey. The experience of the saints who have gone before us can give us some helpful suggestions on how we can remain present to God and nurture companionship with God.

7 FACING THE HEAD WINDS

A retreat experience inevitably leads to new insight, understanding, and changes in commitment. Paying attention to God alone and listening for God's voice alone is certain to release God's transforming power within us. We know that we are different people than we were when we began our retreat. New life has been born within us and we are not the same.

But the world around us has not kept pace with the changes within us. Consequently, when we reenter our daily routine with colleagues, friends, and family, we may discover several barriers to our own growth—barriers that are as formidable for retreat leaders as they are for other participants.

MISUNDERSTANDING BY OTHERS

The first barrier is that we may be misunderstood. What we experience as new faith may be seen as arrogance or a "holier-than-thou" attitude by those observing the persons who have returned from retreat. Since our experience with God is unique and fresh, we may be tempted to try to share too much of our experience with those who are not ready to receive it.

This does not mean that we should be silent about signs of new life. It does mean that we should be prepared to witness to the grace experienced in our own lives with an extra measure of humility and gentleness. It means that we will want to listen as carefully to those around us as we have listened for the voice of God. And then after listening, we should pay attention to what we hear as we seek to give a faithful witness to God's transforming work within us.

Of course, we will want to share out of our rich retreat experience with those around us, but this sharing can often be more effective after we have pondered the events of the retreat and allowed our new life to blossom and grow.

SERVING AS A THREAT TO OTHERS

The second barrier may also be the result of our new life. We now see the world through new eyes, and what was acceptable before may now be unacceptable. What we once criticized may now be seen with greater tolerance. The new life within us is showing outside of us in dramatic ways, as it should. But sometimes this can be threatening to family, friends, colleagues, and the rest of the congregation.

RETURNING TO THE PATTERNS OF THE PAST

And this naturally leads to the third barrier to our continued growth—our desire to conform to what we were and what others expect us to be. While it is important to be patient and ponder the new life within with great humility, it is also important to confess and honor, without embarrassment, this new life as a gift from God.

The pressure to conform to the patterns, values, and expectations of the congregation are strong. There are those who will always want to "press you into their mold," and it is often easier to comply than to resist. Christians believe that God's grace is sufficient to "save us from" taking on the image of the world and "save us for" taking on the image of Christ.

The pressures of family and job-related activities can make it difficult for us to remember who we are and what has happened to us. Family members, colleagues, and our work may make extra demands upon us. Pastors and lay leaders may be even more vulnerable at this point. They are such public figures. Changes in their patterns of ministry will be noticed, not always understood or appreciated, and sometimes criticized.

Therefore, it is important for spiritual leaders to nurture the gifts they have received and to provide the guidance and care of the soul needed by those entrusted to their care.

Old fears and habits will likely make themselves known to us and seek to rob us of the transformation that has taken place within us. New commitments will be challenged by the many voices that seek to guide us back to an older and less-focused discipleship. At this point we realize that the major battles we face are not external but internal. Our experience is not unlike that of the disciples of Jesus in their effort to reach their destination.

The Gospel of Mark tells of the disciples' experience of facing the head winds. Immediately after feeding the five thousand, Jesus sent the disciples to the other side of the sea by boat and he went to the mountain to pray. There is wisdom in this text for retreat leaders and retreat participants. Retreat leaders need recovery and nurture time after every retreat as do those on retreat with them. Jesus needed time alone with God. So do we.

Mark tells us that after the disciples returned from their mission and reported what had happened, Jesus invited them to a lonely place for rest and retreat. But soon the crowds found the lonely place, and Jesus and the disciples were thrust into a ministry of caring that they had not anticipated. The crowd was large, the hour was late, and everyone was hungry. After everyone was fed, the disciples followed the direction that Jesus gave and boarded their boat for the trip across the lake (Mark 6:32-45).

But the wind was strong and the text says that it was against them. They were not making any progress when suddenly Jesus came to them walking on the churning water. They were terrified until they recognized it was Jesus. He told them not to be afraid, got into the boat with them, and the storm lost its fury (Mark 6:47-52).

The disciples had just finished a retreat and had just experienced the miracle of feeding the five thousand. But when the winds came up, they forgot the miracle and concentrated on the storm. The rest, the renewal, the intimacy with Jesus were all forgotten; fear replaced their faith and the memory of this time alone with God.

The temptation to do the same will be present for all who have been on retreat. The head winds are sure to come. We can expect them, but we need not fear them. Rather than fearing them, we may claim them as an opportunity to invite Christ into our "boat" to face the head winds together. When the fears come, or the demands seem too much, or misunderstanding rears its head, remember each of these "head winds" as an opportunity to invite Christ into the experience with you. God is with you and able to provide guidance for your daily routine, as he guided you on retreat.

Pastors and other leaders will want to be especially attentive to the experiences of those returning from retreat. Recognize the special needs and opportunities that follow a spiritual life retreat. Invite those on retreat to share their experience with you and then offer support and continued spiritual guidance. This will be easier if you have been the retreat leader or on retreat with them. Either way, this will mean a continuation of your ministry as spiritual guide and companion on the life of faithfulness.

8 Conserving the Gift

The Christian life flourishes in community. Corporate worship, study, fellowship, and action are the soil in which authentic faith takes root and grows toward maturity. Thus the entire congregation is extremely important in conserving and nurturing the new life that was given birth on retreat. Spiritual leadership by pastor and laity can either conserve, nurture, and build upon this new life or ignore it and permit it to wither and die.

The time following a retreat is a critical period for those who seek to live faithfully. If the gifts received are ignored or denied, they will certainly disappear. Thus congregational life, the routine activities of the congregation, the mission of the congregation, and the leadership of the congregation have a special role to play in conserving the gifts received and guiding the person who has experienced retreat on a path of continued growth.

A number of places where persons on retreat experience the spiritual life of the congregation—such as worship, teaching, administration, mission, and fellowship—deserve special attention.

Worship is one of the most profound experiences of life for humankind. For Christians, gathering around the Lord's Table, the baptismal font, and the scriptures are essential elements of an authentic life of worship. The congregation where scripture, liturgy, music, persons in quest of communion with God, and spirit-filled leadership come together will provide nurture and sustenance to all who experience its life.

Such a community of faith will be a welcome home for those who have been on retreat. For in such an environment new life in Christ is expected, honored, affirmed, strengthened, and then invested in the mission of the congregation.

Worship that is realistic about the demands of daily life in our world and equally realistic about the transcendent and immanent God will speak to everyone and will have special relevance to those who have been awakened anew to the call of God. Pastors and lay leaders will want to incorporate some of the elements of retreat into the worship experiences of the congregation.

Declaration of the truth that worship is determined by the God we seek and the God seen most clearly in Jesus Christ invites us into intimate communion and awaits our response. Liturgy that gives careful guidance for reflection on the scriptures, silence, and guidance in exploring the many methods of prayer, and expectancy that God will act in our lives and the life of the congregation can turn dull and boring worship into life-giving encounters with the living God.

A young woman approached me to seek guidance in her search for a community of faith for herself and her family. We talked about the many options open to everyone in nearly every community. I soon knew that I was talking to someone on a serious quest for God. She talked about the irrelevance of worship that is simply cute and entertaining. It did not feed her soul. She spoke of the endless announcements of every conceivable program from weight loss to dancing and the emptiness that none of this could fill. She spoke of her yearning for God and her desire to have her family incorporated into Christian community. It was clear that she was ready to sacrifice for such a community of faith.

The last time we talked she was still searching for the worshiping community where communion with God is the central goal and everything else supports that goal. I am convinced that she is not alone in her yearning and that the number like her is larger than leaders of the congregation realize. Persons who return from retreat will be able to recognize and name their hunger for God and will be more serious than ever in seeking the bread that satisfies our hunger for God.

One final word about worship: It must not be divorced from real life or from intellectual honesty. Life is demanding and the consequences of sin are real and painful. To deny the reality of the world in which we live is to make worship irrelevant. Many carry burdens that no one can carry alone. They desperately need and eagerly wait to hear of and appropriate the easy yoke of Christ.

Authentic and "saving" worship is set in the midst of the real world and yet remains "not of the world" as it connects the participants to the living God and the communion of saints.

It is also important for the spiritual leader to recognize and convey that there is mystery in our worship—mystery that is forever beyond us and mystery that is awe-inspiring, knee-bending, and hope-giving. As Christians we believe in a God for whom all things are possible (Luke 1:37).

It is also important that spiritual leaders know, demonstrate, and convey the truth that we do not sacrifice our intellectual powers when we intentionally come into the presence of God. Authentic worship demands the very best of all of the powers of life that we can bring. Our minds are gifts from God and are to be invested in our worship of God.

The importance of worship that nurtures and feeds the whole person cannot be overemphasized because it is the one place of nurture and grace most accessible to the greatest number and variety of people.

Years ago I was consulting with a congregation about their future. In a large gathering, to which all members had been invited, the question was raised, "What would you most like your congregation to do for you?"

Much to everyone's surprise, the answer from one person was, "Teach me to pray." This older adult said she had been baptized at the altar of the church, confirmed there, married there, saw her own children baptized and confirmed there, and held her husband's memorial service there. Yet, in all of those experiences and in all of those years, no one had ever taught her how to pray.

Of course, we could say that she could have been learning to pray on her own, and I am sure she did. But the point was well made. We often fail to give Christians adequate tools to cultivate their relationship with God or to live as faithful disciples. The inheritance that belongs to every Christian is frequently left unclaimed. So many of us live a poverty-stricken spiritual life.

Regular classes on prayer that teach a variety of methods and provide a variety of experiences of prayer are a vital part of any ministry that desires to feed the hungry hearts of members, visitors, and friends.

Many have not been taught the most elementary lessons of Bible study or of prayer. Learning to listen for the voice of God in all of life is a discipline infrequently employed. And learning to discriminate among all the voices clamoring for our attention is a forgotten gift. Consequently, the rich spiritual gifts that God is eager to give often go unrecognized and unclaimed.

Congregations that teach these disciplines and help persons cultivate their own capacity to hear and respond to the voice of God will offer a life-giving way for those fortunate enough to be touched by their ministry. The resource section at the end of this guide provides a listing of tools to assist you in your ministry of teaching in these areas.

Small groups have often played a key role in providing nurture and sustenance for persons seeking to live as faithful disciples of Jesus Christ. Covenant Discipleship is a program designed to provide a safe place where Christians can help each other in their daily walk with God. Some Sunday school classes or Bible study and prayer groups may also serve this purpose.

If your congregation does not have such groups, it will be important to create them. The knowledge that anyone may meet weekly for prayer, confession, affirmation, and guidance with others who are serious about their walk with God can offer great encouragement to spiritual development. To know that others are praying for me every day and to be involved praying for others every day is in itself a very positive and formative experience.

As a judicatory leader of a major denomination, I have been involved in the deployment of hundreds of pastors to hundreds of congregations. A vast majority of those congregations listed spiritual leadership as a primary quality in the pastor they desired. Many would have been hard pressed to define precisely what they wanted, but they could recognize it when they experienced it.

For many church members, the age, gender, and race of their spiritual leaders were inconsequential; they wanted unqualified commitment to Christ and the capacity to lead their congregation in that direction. They wanted to know that their pastor was on a spiritual quest and could help them with their own relationship with God and could help them get in touch with their own spiritual journey.

Every pastor and every layperson who leads from a central quest for, commitment to, and companionship with Jesus Christ is a spiritual leader. And spiritual leadership is what the congregation needs and longs for. When it is present, persons on retreat and other members will have their souls nurtured and will discover anew the bread that gives life. It is this kind of leadership that always asks these questions:

- What does God desire for this congregation?
- How is Jesus Christ in this decision?
- What does Jesus Christ call us to be and do?
- Am I seeking God's will above all else in every decision I (we) make and in all that I (we) do?

To lead always from a growing commitment to and companionship with Jesus Christ is to provide the spiritual leadership needed by everyone who seeks to walk with God.

9 DISCOVERING, DEVELOPING, AND DEPLOYING SPIRITUAL LEADERS

Congregations seek spiritual leadership qualities in their pastors, and rightly so. But a pastor soon recognizes the futility of trying to be the only spiritual leader in the congregation. The need is too great and every pastor's gifts, energy, and time are limited. Consequently, it quickly becomes apparent that one of the most important tasks that spiritual leadership must undertake is the discovery, development, and deployment of other spiritual leaders throughout the congregation.

Why discuss this issue here? Because those who have been on retreat are often well on the way toward becoming spiritual leaders. Their own yearning for God has been identified, and they have made at least a preliminary response. Not only has their quest for God been identified; they have also declared a readiness to be formed into the image of Christ.

Many of those who go on retreat have already demonstrated their readiness to become spiritual leaders within the life of the congregation. Therefore, retreats often provide a significant pool of self-selected persons well along the way to becoming spiritual leaders for the congregation.

If those who return from retreat discover (with help by the professional staff and congregation) how to integrate their newfound experience with Christ into everyday life, how to live from their own spiritual center, they will have further demonstrated their capacity to lead from their own spiritual center. Their presence as formal or informal leaders can transform the congregation into a more faithful community.

Retreats are an excellent field for the discovery of spiritual leaders for the congregation. They are also an excellent field for the development of spiritual leaders for the congregation. The vast majority of persons who experience spiritual retreat report renewed faith, hope, commitment, and love for God and neighbor. Most discover a new wholeness, balance, and integration in their lives. Many report not only the desire but demonstrate the experience of living every day from a new spiritual center.

These are the persons who can be recruited to provide the spiritual leadership needed throughout the congregation. They should not be chosen carelessly, for not everyone who goes on retreat is ready to provide spiritual leadership. But from this pool of persons the congregation can carefully and prayerfully select persons for the specific leadership needs that exist.

In seeking to develop spiritual leadership for the congregation, it is wise to provide a retreat experience for the various committees of the congregation. On retreat, the emphasis can more easily be kept on Jesus Christ rather than on program or budget. There is great value in a planning retreat which emphasizes nurturing the spiritual life and planning as a secondary activity.

The retreat designs in the third section of this guide can lend themselves to this kind of planning experience. Development of spiritual leaders will never be fully completed, because the spiritual life is not a final destination. Both are a journey and are never fully completed.

Spiritual leaders can most readily be discovered, developed, and deployed in a retreat setting. If you want your congregation to be Spirit-led, begin planning now for regular retreat experiences for every group and every person in your congregation's sphere of influence!

Part III

Retreat Designs

CONSIDERATIONS WHEN DESIGNING A RETREAT

Creating a time frame for the retreat is a good place to begin. Determine the date and length of the retreat. Then, in light of the purpose, begin to allot time to each segment of the retreat design.

Things to think about include what the content is to be and how it is to be presented, what place plenary sessions, small groups, dyads, and triads, personal reflection time, silence, worship, and solitude should have in the retreat design. Also to be considered should be a significant block of time for closure of the retreat experience and opportunity for evaluation.

To ask the following simple questions can give important insight for the next retreat.

- What went well?
- What was most helpful?
- What did not go well?
- What was least helpful?
- What changes would you suggest?
- What retreat themes would you like to be considered for our next retreat?
- If you could make one suggestion to improve our retreat, what would it be?

Choose several of the questions above or create your own questions to be included on the evaluation instrument. Encourage each participant to complete the evaluation form and leave it at the retreat site.

The following pages include a wide variety of retreat designs. Each one is prepared in such a way that it can be used "off the shelf" as it is or can be modified and adapted to fit a particular situation. The simplest is a three-hour small-group retreat, and the most complex is a church-wide retreat. These retreat models will help you design a retreat for a particular group, event, issue, or theme. Additional help may be found in the resource section at the end of this guide.

The first design is for an all-church retreat. It is designed for two overnights, but it can be adapted to almost any time frame. For instance, the four themes used in this retreat design could easily become four Saturday morning or Sunday evening retreats. You will find an example of this design on pages 71–76.

This design includes a time schedule with suggested activities throughout the time frame, themes, scripture references, and questions for reflection and discussion. The design intends that the retreat leadership provide the lecture/sermon content based on the theme and scripture suggested for each segment of the retreat.

The retreat leader/design team may wish to vary the time allotted to the various segments of the retreat. The time allotted for individual reflection, group discussions, and plenary discussions can be adjusted to meet the purpose of the retreat and the perceived needs of the group more adequately.

If possible, child care should be provided for toddlers and babies. Providing child care will make it possible for many more persons to participate in the retreat and insure that parents are "fully present" for the retreat agenda.

Older children and young people will have activities appropriate to their age group. Although they may appropriately participate in every session, the lecture/sermon, worship, recreation, and fellowship periods may be most accessible to them. Your insight and the purpose of the retreat will help to determine how extensively you want to plan for the various age groups.

The first design is an example of a dialogical retreat. It can be adapted and used as a retreat for men, women, couples, singles, college students, or young people. With more adaptation this design could be used with junior high groups. Younger children can best be served by different design, similar to the suggestions for children included in the all-church retreat.

The design for a youth retreat (see Design #2, pp. 77–86) is an example of a preached/taught retreat. This may be the most common retreat used with young people. However, it would be a mistake to assume that young people are unable to participate fully in other retreat designs. With proper preparation and leadership, a private retreat can be a wonderful avenue of growth for every person, regardless of age.

The third design (see Design #3, pp. 87–90) is for a retreat for older adults. We are often more ready to consider our spiritual life as we approach our older adult years. Some have called this part of life our "wisdom years." It is a time when we have a more realistic understanding of our own mortality. By this time competition and success are often diminished factors in life. As we grow older we are learning to live with the limitations that life brings to all—limitations that have always been there, but may seem more dramatic in our mature years. In short, it is a wonderful time to "come apart to rest and pray." A time for companionship with God and preparation for faithful living with God is as important to this age group as to any other.

Older adults want their lives to make a difference. Do not assume that older adults are no longer ready or willing to act. Give opportunity to each person to invest retreat learnings and experiences in everyday living and in leadership in the congregation. This age group may be your congregation's greatest spiritual leadership resource. To recognize, nurture, and deploy this resource has great potential for transformation of the community of faith.

The next design (see Design #4, pp. 91–102) is intended to model a personally guided retreat. This retreat is more likely to be effective with persons who have had some previous retreat experience. The large blocks of time for reflection, reading, and prayer are especially welcomed by introverts. Extroverts may need more assurance and guidance from leadership for this retreat model.

Design #5 (see pp. 103–108) is intended to be utilized as a private retreat. This design features enough resources to provide content for the entire retreat. Individuals who do not have access to any of the other retreat models because of circumstances can find the spiritual nourishment and guidance needed for daily living in a private retreat. Again, the design will reflect the purpose of the retreat. If the purpose is to find direction, the design will be different than if the purpose is to find spiritual nourishment for daily living.

The sixth design is for an action retreat (see pp. 109–113). The name sounds like an oxymoron, but I think you will see it as a very appropriate design for planning groups or committees which are ready to be more fully engaged in ministry. While the other retreats tend to focus on personal needs and direction, this retreat focuses on the needs of others. The focus may be as close as members of the congregation, the community in which we live and witness, or it may be on the other side of the world.

The design is intended to magnify truths that are present in every retreat, and these are: (1) love for neighbor is second only to love for God in the life of the faithful Christian, (2) God is eager to companion every Christian, and (3) God is able to guide and provide for every individual, group, and congregation.

RETREAT DESIGNS

DESIGN #1: A CHURCH-WIDE RETREAT

"COME AWAY AND REST — A TIME APART"
[Mark 6:31]

AN ALL-CHURCH SPIRITUAL LIFE RETREAT
for
SAINT LUKE COMMUNITY CHURCH
Anytown, U.S.A.

DESERT HILLS RETREAT CENTER

*When your life is more and more
becoming a prayer,
you notice that you are always busy
converting yourself.*
—Henri J. M. Nouwen[4]

DAY ONE

Thus we affirm that in spirituality we have to do with God, not just God in general but with a particular God whose name has been given to us. Spirituality consists in the practice of our humanity in ways appropriate to the God with whom we have to do.

— Walter Brueggemann

3:00–5:00	Gathering/Registration/Getting Settled
5:30	Evening Meal
6:15	Welcome and Announcements

6:30	Worship/Prayer
	    Theme: *Come Aside and Rest*
	    Scripture: Mark 6:30-32

7:00	Presentation/Activity
	    Theme: *Chosen*
	    Scripture: Ephesians 1
	              Isaiah 42:1-4
	              John 15:12-17

Lecture/Sermon on Theme (20 minutes)

Questions for Small Groups and Plenary on the Theme:
- Have you ever felt "chosen"? Describe how it felt.
- How are we "chosen in Christ"?
- What does it mean to you to be "chosen in Christ"?

Small Groups (50 minutes)

Plenary (20 minutes)
    (Note that this design is for adults. Other groups will have a separate design.)

DAY ONE (continued)

8:30   Fellowship/Recreation/Snacks

9:30   Night Prayers

10:15   Rest, Reading, and Reflection

Spirituality is simply our walk with God as God is made known to us in Jesus Christ.

— Rueben P. Job

END OF DAY ONE

A PRAYER FOR THE END OF THE DAY

Blessed are you, O Lord, the God of our fathers, creator of the changes of day and night, giving rest to the weary, renewing the strength of those who are spent, bestowing upon us occasions of song in the evening. As you have protected us in the day that is past, so be with us in the coming night; keep us from every sin, every evil, and every fear; for you are our light and salvation, and the strength of our life. To you be glory for endless ages.

— From *The Book of Common Prayer*

DAY TWO

A life without a lonely place, that is, a quiet center, easily becomes destructive.

— Henri J. M. Nouwen[5]

7:30	Personal/Family Prayer and Reflection/ Nature Walk/Exercise
8:00	Breakfast
9:00	Morning Prayers
9:30	Presentation/Activity

Theme: *Called*

Scripture: Isaiah 42:6-9
Romans 1:1-7
John 10:1-10

Lecture/Sermon (20 minutes)

Questions for Personal Reflection; Small Groups and Plenary Discussion:

- What do you think of when you hear the word *called?*
- How have you felt called during your life?
- How do you think God is calling today?

Personal Reflection (40 minutes)

10:30	Break
11:00	Small Groups (20 minutes)

Plenary (40 minutes)

11:45–1:00	Lunch
1:00–2:00	Silence/Rest

DAY TWO (continued)

2:00   Presentation/Activity

         Theme: *Sent*

         Scripture: Exodus 3:7-12

                  Isaiah 6:1-8

                  John 1:6-8

                  Luke 9:1-6

      Questions for Personal, Small Group, and Plenary Reflection:

- Can you think of anyone whom you believe was sent by God?
- What are the characteristics of those sent by God?
- How are we being sent today?
- What can our congregation do to become more obedient to God's sending?

      Lecture/Sermon (20 minutes)

      Small Groups (45 minutes)

3:00   Break

3:30   Plenary Discussion

4:15   Free Time until Dinner

5:30   Dinner

7:00   Talent Show, Movie, or All-Church Recreation, Games, Nature Walk, etc.

9:00   Snacks

9:45   Evening Prayers

10:30   Rest/Reading

END OF DAY TWO

DAY THREE

Remind yourself often, "I am pure capacity for God; I can be more."

— Macrina Wiederkehr[6]

7:30	Personal/Family Prayer and Reflection/ Nature Walk/ Exercise
8:00	Breakfast
9:00	Morning Prayers
9:30	Presentation/Activity

Theme: *Sustained*

Scripture: Exodus 16:1-21
Psalm 127:1-2
Matthew 15:32-39

Questions for Personal, Small Group, and Plenary Reflection:
- What is your greatest need?
- How would you like God to provide?
- What can you do to help answer your prayer?
- What is the greatest need of your church?
- What can you do to answer that need?

Lecture/Sermon (20 minutes)

Small Groups (20 minutes)

Plenary (20 minutes)

10:00	Break
10:30	Closing Worship/Eucharist

Theme: *Twelve Baskets Full*

Scripture: Matthew 14:13-21

12:00	Lunch (include time for evaluation/witness)

It is comforting and encouraging to remember that God guides and sustains our every step throughout our journey of life.

RETREAT ENDS

DESIGN #2: A YOUTH RETREAT

"CHOSEN FOR LIFE"

A RETREAT DESIGN FOR SENIOR HIGH YOUTH

of

SAINT LUKE COMMUNITY CHURCH
Anytown, U.S.A.

~

5:00 p.m. Friday until 12:00 noon Sunday

Held at
DESERT HILLS RETREAT CENTER

GUIDELINES FOR A YOUTH RETREAT

Every youth group, as every congregation, has its own character and unique quality. Some are small, others large, some urban or suburban, and others rural. Others have trained youth leaders and others struggle to get by with the limited leadership the over-scheduled pastor is able to give. The following design can be adapted to fit each of the above unique abilities of your youth group.

Once again, the leader, lay or clergy, will be the most important element that you can bring to a youth retreat. Listen carefully to what the real concerns of your youth are, rather than listening only to the surface conversation. Design a theme that addresses these deep concerns, and you will provide outstanding ministry to the young people under your leadership and care.

If your youth group is small, you will need a minimum organization for planning and conducting the retreat. However, if your youth group is large, you may want to follow the suggestions for the all-church retreat discussed earlier in this guide. Regardless of the size of the group, involve them in the preparation and the planning. Do not hesitate to consult with parents and grandparents as you seek to determine theme and direction for the retreat.

It will be even more important in a retreat for youth to make this a safe place for every young person. Today many young people have few persons or events that build up their sense of self-worth. Young people, just like adults, need to know they are valued, accepted, loved, and respected as they are. And like adults, they need to be filled with the hope and knowledge that they can become more than they are at the moment.

It will be important to try to get as close to total participation as possible in a youth retreat. There are many reasons for this. One is that every young person will benefit from this time apart. Another is that this may be the best opportunity that a young person will ever have to discover his or her true self, inner life, and potential for meaningful and vital relationship with God. It may also be the best place for young people to learn about and experience the power of the Holy Spirit. And it may be the most likely place where the companionship of Jesus Christ will be discovered, experienced, and practiced.

There is still one more important reason to seek total participation. Retreat settings provide wonderful opportunities to build trust and to bond together as a group. With careful direction by the leader, it is difficult for anyone to feel unwanted, unloved, unaccepted, unworthy, and left out. Sharing food, song, scripture, personal story, prayer, recreation, and silence results in a sense of community that is healthy and strong. The bonding that takes place in retreat often makes it difficult for those not at the retreat to feel included later.

This suggests that the leadership should make every effort to have everyone there. This is also an excellent time to bring guests and visitors into the life of the group. And a final word about those who are not able to participate: Do all you can to include them and help them to feel that they are also "insiders." Try to tell the story of retreat in positive and inviting ways. Prepare those on retreat to avoid the mistakes of exclusiveness when they return.

Incorporate the truths learned at the retreat into the ongoing life of the youth group. This will help you to include those who were unable to be a part of the retreat as well as conserve the values gained.

This is another place to involve parents and guardians. Report accurately and in some detail about the retreat directly or by letter to parents. This can help to further the truths learned and spiritual growth experienced by the young persons themselves. It is also a good way to share the benefit of the retreat with the families of those who have been involved.

The retreat that follows is designed for two overnights, but it can be easily adapted to several one-day retreats or to a series of three-hour retreats.

DAY ONE

Every human being is of incredible worth regardless of the circumstance of race, gender, social distinctions, natural gifts of appearance, intelligence, or physical skills. You are loved, valued, and accepted just as you are and God looks upon you with favor because you are a part of God's magnificent creation.

3:00-5:00   Gathering/Registration/Getting Settled
        If the retreat is conducted away from home, have persons available to assist participants to find their room and get settled. Prepare some participatory games and a worksheet or two that can be used individually to involve those who arrive early.

5:30   Evening Meal

6:15   Welcome and Announcements

6:30   Music and Singing
        This is a place for contemporary and traditional music. If possible, have someone with vocal skills or skills with a guitar or other instrument lead the music and singing.

6:45   Worship/Prayer
        For this first session it may be necessary for the leader or other adults to lead this experience. However, as soon as possible get the youth involved in providing leadership in the worship experiences.

7:15   Presentation: *"Who Is God?"*

DAY ONE (continued)

7:45   Personal Reflection
- What is my earliest memory about God?
- How have my ideas about God changed?
- Complete the statement, "God is . . ." with your own understanding about God today.
- Write out your response to the questions and be prepared to share some of your insights with one or two other persons when asked to do so.

8:00   Sharing Insights in Dyads or Triads
Two or three persons are asked to share some of the insights that came during the personal reflection on the presentation and suggested questions.

8:15   Plenary Discussion
- What new insights have you gained?
- How do you feel about the insights gained?
- What questions remain?

Leadership will want to make certain that even radical ideas and strange questions are given attention. This may be a good place to expand on some of the ideas expressed or be prepared to share a portion of your own witness.

8:45   Recreation/Activities
It is important to have activities planned in which all can participate. Some may enjoy physical activity while others would prefer or are more able to participate in more sedentary games. Softball, basketball, volleyball, soccer, and jogging may be just right for everyone. But be especially sensitive to those for whom such activities are unpleasant or impossible.

DAY ONE (continued)

10:15   Snacks/Fellowship

              Try to have fresh fruits and popcorn as well as the more traditional snacks.

10:45   Night Prayer

              Involve young persons in leadership in the worship and prayer experiences as soon as possible.

11:00   Silence

              While the first night may not be the best time to enter the "Great Silence," it is something you may want to include at some point in the retreat. If the group is not ready for silence until morning prayers, try a silent meal or a significant block of time for silence during the rest of the retreat.

To place one's life into the hands of God is to discover a new confidence and peace.

END OF DAY ONE

BE PRESENT AT OUR TABLE, LORD

Be present at our table, Lord;
Be here and everywhere adored;
Thy creatures bless, and grant that we
May feast In paradise with thee.[7]

DAY TWO

The beauty, wonder, and grandeur of the world within is often forsaken for the noise and glitter of the world around us.

7:30   Personal Prayer and Reflection/Early Morning Walk

8:00   Breakfast

9:00   Presentation/Activity
        Lecture: *"Who Am I?"*

9:20   Personal Reflection, for "your eyes only"

        Finish the statements:
        - I am a child of God with the following characteristics . . .
        - I find my self-worth in . . .
        - I would like to be . . .

9:30   Small Group Discussion
        - How can we value, affirm each other?
        - How can we help each to remember who we really are?

10:00   Break

10:30   Plenary Discussion
        - What have you learned about each other?
        - What have you learned about yourself?
        - Name three of life's most important qualities.
        - What can the church do to help us discover and affirm our true identity?

11:00   Keeping a Journal
        Each participant is invited to write out his or her response to the experience of the retreat thus far and then write a prayer expressing thanksgiving, petition, and intercession.

DAY TWO (continued)

11:45	Lunch
1:00	Recreation: Swimming/Ball Games/Hiking/ Bird Watching/Skiing
5:30	Dinner
7:00	Talent Show or Movie Followed by Discussion
9:00	Plenary Discussion

- What did we learn about ourselves?
- What did we learn about others?
- What changes would we like to see in each other and in ourselves?

9:30	Snacks
10:15	Night Prayers
11:00	Silence until Breakfast Tomorrow

END OF DAY TWO

THIS IS THE DAY THE LORD HATH MADE

This is the day the Lord hath made;
He calls the hours his own.
Let heaven rejoice, let earth be glad,
And praise surround the throne.[8]

DAY THREE

Each new day comes as a gift from God's hand designed just for you. Remember to thank God for the gift!

7:30	Personal Prayers, Nature Walk, Quiet Reflection
8:00	Breakfast
9:00	Presentation/Activity Lecture: *"Who Are We Together?"*
9:20	Personal Reflection • What do I want from this community (group)? • What can I do to strengthen our youth group?
9:45	Plenary Discussion • How do we live together and affirm each other's identity and strengthen our community? • What are some benefits of community? • What are some responsibilities for community? • What will we do to strengthen our community and our walk with God?
10:15	Break
10:45	Closing Worship/Eucharist If the retreat is held in or near the place where the rest of the congregation is at worship, consider joining them for this period. When possible, conclude with a closing commitment/communion service.
11:30	Evaluation • What did I like most about the retreat? • What did I like least about the retreat? • What changes would have made the retreat better?

11:45   Lunch

God is able to provide for all of our needs every day.
Have you talked to God about those needs today?

END OF RETREAT

DESIGN #3: AN OLDER ADULT RETREAT

"CELEBRATING THE SECOND HALF OF LIFE"

AN OLDER ADULT ONE-DAY RETREAT

for members of

SAINT LUKE COMMUNITY CHUCH
Anytown, U.S.A.

Held at
DESERT HILLS RETREAT CENTER

SUGGESTED OUTLINE: AN OLDER ADULT RETREAT

8:30   Gathering, Registration, and Fellowship
        Continental breakfast with fruit and beverages is an option. Otherwise, have beverages available as people gather.

9:00   Welcome/Introduction of Theme/Process of the Day

9:15   Morning Worship/Prayers

        Ask participants to share personal prayer requests.

9:30   Presentation/Activity

        Lecture/Movie/Panel on the Theme:
        "God's Chosen Vessels"

        Scripture: 2 Thessalonians 2:13-17
                   Deuteronomy 6:7-11
                   Genesis 17:1-8
                   Ephesians 2:1-10

10:00   Break — Fresh fruit and beverages

10:30   Small Groups of Five to Seven Persons

        Questions for Reflection:
        • In what sense do I feel chosen?
        • How is God seeking to draw me close today?
        • How is God seeking to bless my life today?
        • How is God seeking to use my life today?

11:00   Plenary
        • What affirmations were discovered?
        • What insights emerged?
        • What questions remain?

11:15   Break

11:30   Lunch

12:15   Presentation/Activity

Lecture/Movie/Panel on the Theme:
"Growing with Limitations"

Scripture: Deuteronomy 3:23-39
John 21:15-18

12:40   Questions for Personal Reflection:

- What are some of the limitations I experience?
- How do limitations provide opportunity to grow in my faith, relationship to God, and to others?
- What opportunity for growth am I thankful for today?

1:00   Presentation/Activity

Lecture/Movie/Panel on the Theme:
"God is Able to Provide"

Scripture: Isaiah 40:1-2
Ephesians 6:10-17
John 14:15-18
John 14:18-24
Ephesians 3:14-21

2:00   Personal Reflection Time
Each person is asked to write a brief response to each question and be prepared to share with the small group later.

Questions for Reflection/Discussion:

- What are some of the ways God has provided for you in the past?
- What are some of the ways God is providing for you today?
- What are the ways in which you desire God to provide for you today?

2:30   Small Groups of Five to Seven Persons
Discuss response to questions above.

2:45   Plenary Discussion

3:00   Closing Communion/Commitment

⌒

God is with us in all of this life and all of the life to come. We have nothing to fear and much to celebrate as God's beloved children. Thanks be to God.

RETREAT ENDS

DESIGN #4: A PERSONALLY GUIDED RETREAT

"WALKING WITH CHRIST"

A PERSONALLY GUIDED RETREAT

for members of

SAINT LUKE COMMUNITY CHURCH
Anytown, U.S.A.

Held at
DESERT HILLS RETREAT CENTER

GUIDELINES FOR A PERSONALLY GUIDED RETREAT

A personally guided retreat may be for just one person or for up to six persons for each retreat guide or spiritual director. It is a design that works well for those persons who are ready to take more seriously their own spiritual growth. Any committed individual or group in the congregation will benefit from this kind of retreat experience. While the following design calls for a five-day experience, it could be used as a three-day retreat, a one-day retreat, or five weekly retreats.

The retreat design may be built around a biblical passage or a series of passages, or it may be designed around some other spiritual reading. The following design includes a series of biblical passages and readings from the book, *A Simple Path* by Mother Teresa. Refer to the list of additional resources at the end of this guide for other possible readings.

DAY ONE

Morning   Arrival, Getting Settled
> Retreat leader or person responsible for hospitality meets each guest.

Reading Assignment
> Each guest receives materials and the first reading assignment.
>
> Scripture: Luke 6:12-16
>
> *The Simple Path*, Introduction and Chapter One

Corporate Midday Prayers

Lunch Together

Appointments for Personal Consultation
with Each Participant

Afternoon   Personal Consultations with Each Retreatant
> This period is to give the retreat leader an opportunity to learn something about the persons attending and why they are there. While each person will have the same basic readings, it may be important to tailor the readings or add others for each participant.
>
> Silence is maintained by those not in consultation with the retreat leader or a spiritual guide. The following questions for reflection may be assigned to the participants for this first afternoon. Following the individual consultations, the retreat leader may assign more specific questions and activities for each participant.

DAY ONE (continued)

Where do you see yourself in this text?
- As God's personal letter to you, what is God saying to you through this passage?
- What insights for your life have you gained from the Introduction and Chapter One?
- Record your discoveries in your personal journal.

Late Afternoon Exercise: Walking/Swimming/Work on the Grounds/ Volleyball, etc.

Dinner

Evening Brief presentation by the Retreat Leader on the Theme: *"Why Are We Here?"*

Silence and solitude for reflection on the evening theme.

Participants will record their response in personal journals.

Night Prayers Together
    Night prayers are usually led by the retreat leader on the first day.

    On following days, retreatants may be asked to lead.

Silence and Solitude until Morning Prayer

END OF DAY ONE

DAY TWO

Morning

Personal Prayers

Corporate Morning Prayer

Breakfast

Group Discussion on Yesterday's Experience

Brief Presentation on Theme:
"What Do You Want God to do for You?"

Scripture: Luke 18:35-43

Personal Reflection
Each participant spends the rest of the morning in personal reflection on the biblical text. Response is to be recorded in the personal journal being kept.

Corporate Midday Prayer

Lunch

Afternoon

Spiritual Guidance
Participants will meet for thirty minutes with their spiritual guides for guidance and reflection. Appointments for guidance will be arranged at lunch time. Those waiting for their appointment and those who have had their appointment may use the rest of the afternoon for recreation: physical exercise, reading, writing, painting, etc.

Dinner

DAY TWO (continued)

Evening   Evening Assignment
> Read chapter two or specific assignment suggested by guide/retreat leader. Record response in personal journal.

Evening Sharing/Light Snacks and Conversation

Corporate Night Prayers

Silence and Solitude until Morning Prayer

END OF DAY TWO

THE DAY IS PAST AND OVER

The day is past and over;
>   All thanks, O Lord, to thee!
We pray thee that offenseless
>   The hours of dark may be.
O Jesus, keep us in thy sight,
And guard us through the coming night.

Be thou our souls' preserver,
O God, for thou dost know
How many are the perils
>   Through which we have to go.
Lord Jesus Christ, O hear our call,
And guard and save us from them all.[9]

DAY THREE

Morning   Personal Prayer

Corporate Morning Prayer

Breakfast

Set Appointments for Guidance Consultation
    with Each Participant

Group Discussion: *"What Have I Experienced Thus Far?"*

Personal Reflection Time
        Scripture: Matthew 14:13-21

How Are You Being Fed?
• How is God calling you to help feed others?
• Is your basket full?

Book: Chapter Three

Journal Your Responses

Corporate Midday Prayer

Lunch

Afternoon   Continue Personal Reflection and Journaling

Continue Personal Guidance/Consultation
    with Each Participant throughout the Day

Recreation/Physical Exercise
        (As facility and individual capacity permits)

Dinner

DAY THREE (continued)

Evening   Group Discussion: *"What Have I Learned About God and How God is Active in My Life and the World?"*
- What have I learned about others?
- What have I learned about myself?
- How will I incorporate this learning in my daily life?

Sharing Time/Light Snacks

Corporate Night Prayer

Silence and Solitude until Morning Prayer

END OF DAY THREE

ABIDE WITH ME

Swift to its close ebbs out life's little day;
earth's joys grow dim; its glories pass away;
change and decay in all around I see;
O Thou who changest not, abide with me.

I need thy presence every passing hour.
What but thy grace can foil the tempter's power?
Who, like thyself, my guide and stay can be?
Through cloud and sunshine, Lord, abide with me.

I fear no foe, with thee at hand to bless;
ills have no weight, and tears no bitterness.
Where is death's sting? Where, grave, thy victory?
I triumph still, if thou abide with me.[10]

DAY FOUR

Morning   Personal Prayer

Corporate Morning Prayer

Breakfast

Confirm Appointments for Personal Guidance/
  Consultation

Personal Reflection

    Scripture: Matthew 14:22-36

Questions for Reflection:

- How are you being challenged to risk, get out of the boat?
- Where do you see God at work making well those who are being "touched by God"?

Journal Your Responses

Corporate Midday Prayers

Lunch Together

Afternoon   Personal Reflection

Chapter Four in Assigned Book

Personal Guidance and Consultation for Each Participant

Recreation/Physical Exercise

Dinner

DAY FOUR (continued)

Evening   Group Discussion

- What is God saying to me through the scripture of the day?
- What is God saying to me through the assigned book?
- Is there anything you wish to share from your journal?

Sharing Time/Light Snacks

Corporate Night Prayer

Silence and Solitude until Morning Prayer

 END OF DAY FOUR

LET ALL THE PEOPLES PRAISE GOD

May God be gracious to us and bless us
    and make his face to shine upon us,   *Selah*
that your way may be known upon earth,
    your saving power among all nations.
Let the peoples praise you, O God;
    let all the peoples praise you.

Let the nations be glad and sing for joy,
    for you judge the peoples with equity
    and guide the nations upon earth.   *Selah*
Let the peoples praise you, O God;
    let all the peoples praise you.

The earth has yielded its increase;
    God, our God, has blessed us.
May God continue to bless us;
    let all the ends of the earth revere him.
                         — Psalm 67

DAY FIVE

Morning   Personal Prayer

Corporate Morning Prayer

Breakfast

Confirm Consultation/Guidance Sessions
with Each Participant
>> Sessions continue throughout the day.

Presentation by Retreat Leader on Theme:
"Preparing for Reentry"

Personal Reflection Time

> Scripture: Mark 6:45-52

Reflection Questions:

- Will the wind "be against you" as you return to your daily routine?
- How will you prepare for your reentry into your daily routine?
- How do you desire for God to "come to you" as you return?

Read Chapter Five in Assigned Book

Journal Response to Scripture and Reading in Book

Corporate Midday Prayer

Lunch

DAY FIVE (continued)

Afternoon   Presentation: *"Designing a Personal Way of Living"*
- How will I live in order to continue a faithful and growing walk with Jesus Christ?

Personal Time
Each participant designs a "Personal Way of Living," including what will be done daily, weekly, monthly, and annually to continue the journey with Jesus Christ.

Group Discussion
Review retreat experience and provide some time for personal witness.

Closing Communion/Commitment

END OF RETREAT

DESIGN #5: A PRIVATE RETREAT

"LISTENING FOR THE VOICE OF GOD"

A PRIVATE RETREAT

for members of

SAINT LUKE COMMUNITY CHURCH
Anytown, U.S.A.

∽

*Any place where you withdraw
undisturbed for a period of deep communion
    with God
can become a holy place.*

GUIDELINES FOR A PRIVATE RETREAT

The following retreat design can be used by a pastor or professional staff person in the congregation or by anyone with a minimum amount of instruction. The theme may be varied to suit the particular situation of the participant.

While theme and content will vary, the basic outline of the retreat design will remain the same. That is a generous use of silence, prayer, reflective reading of scripture and other spiritual reading, and, where necessary or appropriate, a time for rest and recreation or exercise of some kind.

The design that follows can be used anywhere. It is wise to seek out some location that can become a holy place—a place where disturbances will be at a minimum. Some sites often used are retreat centers, cabins, or state parks. However, private retreats can be held in one's own study, living room, backyard, or even the furnace room! The important thing is the desire to focus all one's attention upon God and only God.

This design also assumes a one-day retreat beginning in the morning and continuing until the next morning. But the retreat could begin at any time during the day and could end at any point in the day. As an option, the design could be adapted and used in several three-hour periods during one week. Ideally, however, this design will be used in one block of time and at some place that has the highest potential of becoming a holy place.

It is assumed that you will take with you for this retreat some healthful food and beverages. Should you choose to fast for the day, be sure to have plenty of water with you and check with your physician before you begin your fast. Some have found a day of silence is a fast from noise such as radio, television, newspapers, and personal interaction with others.

Sometimes the intensity of communion with God and the sudden shift from "busyness" to peaceful quiet can be unnerving and even frightening. Remember that God is with you and will sustain you throughout this time of retreat. It can be a time when you fashion a new companionship with the living Christ that will continue as long as God gives you life.

Because of the factors mentioned above, sleep is sometimes slow in coming. Some people have found that it is good practice to take some exercise about an hour before you intend to go to sleep.

This design can be repeated again and again. Simply build the time around another theme, biblical passage, and other spiritual reading. Or, if you wish to do a two-day retreat, you may repeat the schedule of the day with new spiritual readings (biblical and other).

SUGGESTED OUTLINE: A PRIVATE RETREAT

Morning   Arrival/Getting Settled for the Day
> A period of prayer when the individual asks the Holy Spirit to be the guide for the retreat, offers all of self to God, and invites God's presence into all of the moments of the day.

Silent Listening
> This is a time when the constant prayer is, "Speak Lord, your servant is listening."

Scripture Reading
> Use selected passages supporting the theme, such as:
> > 1 Samuel 3:1-21
> > 1 Kings 19:1-18
> > Acts 9:1-19

> Read the passage you select as though God were speaking directly and personally to you.
> - What is God saying to me?
> - How is God trying to speak to me today?
> - What is my part in establishing and maintaining good communication with God?
> - What are the three major messages in this text for me?
> - After listening and hearing, Samuel, Paul, and Elijah were called to respond to God's message. How am I being called to respond?

Journal Writing
> This is an important aid in discovering and conserving insights.

Prayer
> Prayer will be part of the entire day, but you will want to include large blocks of time for prayer.

Other Spiritual Reading

Select a book or two that supports the theme of the day. For this design use chapter three in Marjorie Thompson's book, *Soul Feast*.

For reflection:

- List all the ways in which God speaks to you. Include those that Marjorie Thompson suggests.
- Which of these "voices of God" do I listen to most frequently?
- Which of these "voices of God" do I hear most easily?
- What changes in my life am I called to make in order to hear God more clearly?

Journal Writing

Record responses to the reflection on the chapter just read.

Rest and Recreation

This is an important ingredient of a helpful time apart. If rest is your great need, place it in your retreat. All of us need physical exercise. Include it in your day. Move around at least every two hours, and if you are able, find at least one hour during the day for strenuous exercise, such as walking, swimming, or chopping wood.

Silent Listening

This is a time when you quieten the voices without and within and free yourself to be as open as possible to God's voice and message. This is not a time to journal, read the Bible or any other text. It is a time to be seated comfortably and give as much of yourself as you are able to give to listening to God's word for you at this moment. It is a time to dismiss gently the concerns of your life as they enter your consciousness and return again to being present to God.

Journal Writing

Record what you have heard in the last time of listening and throughout the day.

Covenant and Commitment

Conclude your retreat time with an affirmation of the covenant with God with which you began your retreat and note any additions for changes. After reflection on your commitments, you may find the careful reading of your favorite Communion Service text as a way of renewing your covenant with God and remembering God's covenant with you.

Closing Prayer

This is a time to place all of the events of the day and as much of your life as you are able into the care of God as you give thanks for these hours of concentrated attentiveness to God.

RETREAT ENDS

DESIGN #6: AN ACTION RETREAT

"SEND ME"

AN ACTION RETREAT

for leaders of

SAINT LUKE COMMUNITY CHURCH
Anytown, U.S.A.

Held at
DESERT HILLS RETREAT CENTER

GUIDELINES FOR AN ACTION RETREAT

The following design can be used in a one-day or three-session retreat with appropriate breaks for rest, meals, and sleep. The design can also be used for three consecutive Sunday afternoons or as many planning meetings. The scripture references and themes may also be changed to fit the occasion and need at the time of the retreat.

No retreat is ever complete without serious consideration of the question, "What is God calling me to do?" Honesty and openness before God always leads to action, personal and corporate. There are times when an entire retreat experience is given to discernment about a course of action to be taken by an individual, a congregation, or groups within the congregation. There are still other times when a retreat is the setting for preparation for a specific action that grows out of our faith in and relationship to God.

A planning retreat for an administrative board, worship committee, or social justice committee can be the setting where wisdom, courage, strength, and guidance are received for some specific faith or action responses in the congregation and in the world. This simple retreat design can give some structure to one's search for and obedience to God's direction.

Jesus saw faith related to all of life and lived out this vision in every aspect of his life and ministry. One cannot read the scriptures without reaching the conclusion that God desires holy living by everyone. Neither can there be any question that this holy living grows out of an unqualified love for God and neighbor.

SUGGESTED OUTLINE: AN ACTION RETREAT

> Cease to do evil,
> learn to do good;
> seek justice,
> rescue the oppressed,
> defend the orphan,
> plead for the widow.
> — Isaiah 1:6b-17

These twelve Jesus sent out with the following instructions: . . . proclaim the good news. . . . Cure the sick, raise the dead, cleanse the lepers, cast out demons
— Matthew 10:5-8

Morning   Arrival and Registration

Gathering

Welcome/Orientation to the Retreat

Worship/Prayer

Sharing of Personal Stories/Getting Acquainted
Even in groups that know each other quite well, it is important to give opportunity to tell and hear one another's story. Sometimes questions similar to the ones listed here can serve to encourage full participation and give some direction to the participants.

Presentation/Lecture I
"Living Faithfully in a Living Church"
Scripture: Matthew 25:1-13

Personal Reflection

- Where do I see myself in this passage?
- What has God said to me in this passage?
- How shall I respond?

Plenary/Small Group Discussion

- What are the insights gleaned thus far?
- What action steps are called forth now?
- To what are we willing to make commitment?

Presentation/Lecture II

"Living Faithfully in a Broken World"
Scripture: Matthew 25:31-44

Personal Reflection

- How does this passage relate to my/our life and ministry?
- What are the urgings I feel when reflecting on this passage?
- Record any commitments that you would like to make.

Small Group/Plenary Discussion

- What new insights, wisdom, direction came during the personal reflection time?
- What are the commitments to action that we are ready to make at this point?

Presentation/Lecture III

"Living with God in the World"
Scripture: Matthew 25:14-30

Plenary Discussion

- What changes are called for as we seek to live with God in the world?
- What changes are we willing to make in order to live more fully with God in the world?
- What kind of help do we need in order to live more faithfully with God in all of life?
- What next steps are we called to take?
- How will our decision be reinforced with courage, wisdom, and strength from God?

Closing Worship/Commitment

RETREAT ENDS

CREATING AND USING A RETREAT CHECKLIST

The checklist on page 117 is an example of some of the things you will need to consider in planning for a successful retreat. The items listed and the suggested time frame can provide some guidance for those responsible for the retreat. Nothing here is set in stone, but experience has proven that it is difficult to plan a successful retreat in a short time. To try to do all of the preparation of congregation, leadership, and setting just before the retreat is certain to lead to frustration for the retreat leadership and a less-than-satisfying experience for the participants.

The checklist on page 117 is designed to be modified for the specific retreat being planned. Feel free to adapt it to fit your needs. Further, you may wish to create your own more complete checklist by following a simple process that is outlined in the next paragraph.

Once you have chosen or created a design for the retreat, look at each activity and ask the following questions:

- Why are we doing this?
- What is needed to accomplish our goal?
- Who is responsible for this activity?
- What resources are needed for this activity?
- What is needed for recreation, small group discussion, breaks, or worship?

By looking at each activity and asking the above questions, you will discover the kind of resourcing that needs to be done.

If your retreat includes many people and utilizes a small group process, you will need small group facilitators. Movie projector, newsprint, pencils, paper, recreation equipment, music leader, piano, or guitar are the kinds of things you may need to complete the activity you have designed.

Be sure to include a time and process for evaluation before people leave the retreat site. The creation of a form is helpful for a large group but may not be necessary for a small group. You may want to create your own evaluation process. Some traditional questions for evaluation are:

- What did you like most about the retreat?
- What did you like least about the retreat?
- What would you like to see changed for the next retreat?"

Your retreat has been designed as a sacred encounter for each participant. All of your preparation and planning should be designed to make sacred encounter possible for the largest number of people. Invite and expect full participation in creating an environment where God can be made known. And always remember, the Holy Spirit is the leader of every spiritual life retreat and seeks to guide and sustain you and those whom you lead.

A RETREAT PLANNING CHECKLIST

Activity	Responsibility	When Needed	Completed
Decide to have retreat	Pastor and lay leadership	Before scheduling	❑
Set dates	Pastor and lay leadership	6 months before retreat	❑
Name planning team	Pastor and lay leadership	6 months before retreat	❑
Promote and pray	Planning team	Continuous	❑
Begin preparation	Congregation	6 months before retreat	❑
Select site	Planning team	6 months before retreat	❑
Select design	Planning team	6 months before retreat	❑
Select leadership	Pastor/Planning team	6 months before retreat	❑
Begin registration	Planning team	5 months before retreat	❑
Create budget and get it approved	Planning team	5 months before retreat	❑
Continue registration	Planning team	5 months before retreat	❑
Select theme	Planning team and pastor	4 months before retreat	❑
Continue registration	Planning team	4 months before retreat	❑
Finalize design	Planning team	3 months before retreat	❑
Organizational details	Planning team	3 months before retreat	❑
Transportation, meals, housing, breaks, worship, recreation, hymnal, etc.	Planning team	3 months before retreat	❑
Continue registration	Planning team	3 months before retreat	❑
Tell story to congregation	Retreat leadership	2 months before retreat	❑
Continue registration	Planning team	2 months before retreat	❑
Brief taste of theme for congregation during worship	Retreat leadership	1 month before retreat	❑
Final appeal for registration	Planning team	1 month before retreat	❑
Conduct retreat	Leadership/Planning team	—	❑
Evaluation	Planning team/Pastor	At conclusion of retreat	❑
Begin planning next retreat	Pastor and lay leadership	Before scheduling	❑

BIBLIOGRAPHY AND ADDITIONAL RESOURCES

Listed below are some additional resources for those leading spiritual life retreats.

Ackerman, John. *Spiritual Awakening: A Guide to Spiritual Life in Congregations.* Bethesda, Md.: The Alban Institute, 1994.

Bondi, Roberta C. *To Love as God Loves: Conversations with the Early Church.* Minneapolis: Augsburg Fortress Publishers, 1987.

Brueggemann, Walter. *Praying the Psalms.* ed. Carl Koch. Winona, Minn.: Saint Mary's Press, 1993.

Byrne, Lavinia, ed. *The Hidden Tradition: Women's Spiritual Writings Rediscovered: An Anthology.* Crossroad, N.Y.: Crossroad Publishing Company, 1991.

Foster, Richard J. *Prayer: Finding the Heart's True Home.* San Francisco: HarperSanFrancisco, 1992.

Groff, Kent Ira. *Active Spirituality: A Guide for Seekers and Ministers.* Bethesda, Md.: The Alban Institute, 1993.

Guenther, Margaret. *Holy Listening: The Art of Spiritual Direction.* Boston: Crowley Publications, 1992.

Job, Rueben P. and Norman Shawchuck. *A Guide to Prayer for All God's People.* Nashville: Upper Room Books, 1990

Job, Rueben P. and Norman Shawchuck. *A Guide to Prayer for Ministers and Other Servants.* 2nd ed. Nashville: Upper Room Books, 1983.

Job, Rueben P. *A Guide to Retreat for All God's Shepherds.* Nashville: Abingdon Press, 1994.

Millard, Kent. *Spiritual Gifts.* Nashville: Abingdon Press, 1994.

Morris, Danny. *Yearning to Know God's Will: A Workbook for Discerning God's Guidance for Your Life.* Grand Rapids, Mich.: Zondervan Publishing Company, 1991.

Mulholland, M. Robert, Jr. *Shaped by the Word: The Power of Scripture in Spiritual Formation.* Nashville: Upper Room Books, 1985.

Teresa, Mother. *A Simple Path.* N.Y.: Ballantine Books, Inc., 1995.

Thompson, Marjorie J. *Soul Feast: An Invitation to the Christian Spiritual Life.* Louisville: Westminster John Knox Press, 1995.

Thurman, Howard. *Deep Is the Hunger.* Richmond, Ind.: Friends United Press, 1973.

Underhill, Evelyn. *Ways of the Spirit.* ed. Grace Adolphsen Brame. 2nd ed. Crossroad, N.Y.: Crossroad Publishing Company, 1993.

Prayers, Hymns, and Meditations for Persons on Retreat

Be Present at Our Table, Lord

Be present at our table, Lord;
be here and everywhere adored;
thy creatures bless,
and grant that we may feast
    in paradise with thee.

— John Cennick, 1742, alt.

Thy Will

Thy will, O Lord, whate'er I do,
    My principle of action be.
Thy will I would through life pursue,
    Impelled, restrained, and ruled by Thee;
And only think, and speak and move,
    As taught and guided by Thy love.

— From a poem by Charles Wesley

LET US MAGNIFY THE LORD

I will bless the LORD at all times;
    his praise shall continually be in my mouth.
My soul makes its boast in the LORD;
    let the humble hear and be glad.
O magnify the LORD with me,
    and let us exalt his name together.

I sought the LORD, and he answered me,
    and delivered me from all my fears.
Look to him, and be radiant;
    so your faces shall never be ashamed.
This poor soul cried, and was heard by the LORD,
    and was saved from every trouble.
The angel of the LORD encamps
    around those who fear him, and delivers them.
O taste and see that the LORD is good;
    happy are those who take refuge in him.
O fear the LORD, you his holy ones,
    for those who fear him have no want.
The young lions suffer want and hunger,
    but those who seek the LORD lack no good thing.

— Psalm 34:1-10

LORD, HEAR MY VOICE!

Out of the depths I cry to you, O LORD.
    LORD, hear my voice!
Let your ears be attentive
    to the voice of my supplications!

If you, O LORD, should mark iniquities,
    LORD, who could stand?
But there is forgiveness with you,
    so that you may be revered.

I wait for the LORD, my soul waits,
    and in his word I hope;
my soul waits for the LORD
    more than those who watch for the
        morning,
    more than those who watch for the
        morning.

O Israel, hope in the LORD!
    For with the LORD there is steadfast
        love,
    and with him is great power to redeem.
It is he who will redeem Israel
    from all its iniquities.

                — Psalm 130

THE EVERLASTING LORD

The LORD is king, he is robed in majesty;
    the LORD is robed, he is girded with
        strength.
He has established the world; it shall never
        be moved;
    your throne is established from of old;
    you are from everlasting.

The floods have lifted up, O LORD,
    the floods have lifted up their voice;
    the floods lift up their roaring.
More majestic than the thunders of mighty
        waters,
    more majestic than the waves of the
        sea,
    majestic on high is the LORD!

Your decrees are very sure;
    holiness befits your house,
    O LORD, forevermore.

— Psalm 93

PRAYER OF JOHN CHRYSOSTOM

Almighty God,
you have given us grace at this time
    with one accord to make our common supplication to you;
and you have promised through your well-loved Son
    that when two or three are gathered together in his name,
        you will be in the midst of them.
Fulfill now, O Lord, our desires and petitions
    as may be best for us;
        granting us in this world knowledge of your truth,
        and in the age to come life everlasting.

A COVENANT PRAYER

I am no longer my own, but thine.
Put me to what thou wilt, rank me with whom thou wilt.
Put me to doing, put me to suffering.
Let me be employed by thee or laid aside for thee,
exalted for thee or brought low for thee.
Let me be full, let me be empty.
Let me have all things, let me have nothing.
I freely and heartily yield all things
to thy pleasure and disposal.
And now, O glorious and blessed God,
Father, Son, and Holy Spirit,
thou art mine, and I am thine. So be it.
And the covenant which I have made on earth,
let it be ratified in heaven.[11]

IN THE VOICE OF LOVE

Not in the strong impetuous wind
Can I my gentle Saviour find;
Not in a hurricane of sound
Which rends the rocks, and shakes the ground;

Not in the heaven-enkindled fire,
The fervours of intense desire;
But I expect Him from above,
In the soft whispering voice of love.

— From a poem by Charles Wesley

THE KING OF GLORY

The earth is the Lord's and all that is in it,
    the world, and those who live in it;
for he has founded it on the seas,
    and established it on the rivers.

Who shall ascend the hill of the Lord?
    And who shall stand in his holy place?
Those who have clean hands and pure
        hearts,
    who do not lift up their souls to what is
        false,
    and do not swear deceitfully.
They will receive blessing from the Lord,
    and vindication from the God of their
        salvation.
Such is the company of those who seek
        him,
    who seek the face of the God of Jacob.
                                Selah

Lift up your heads, O gates!
    and be lifted up, O ancient doors!
    that the King of glory may come in.
Who is the King of glory?
    The Lord, strong and mighty,
    the Lord, mighty in battle.
Lift up your heads, O gates!
    and be lifted up, O ancient doors!
    that the King of glory may come in.
Who is this King of glory?
    The Lord of hosts,
    he is the King of glory.   *Selah*

                          — Psalm 24

How Great Are God's Works

It is good to give thanks to the Lord,
    to sing praises to your name, O Most High;
to declare your steadfast love in the morning,
    and your faithfulness by night,
to the music of the lute and the harp,
    to the melody of the lyre.
For you, O Lord, have made me glad by your work;
    at the works of your hands I sing for joy.

How great are your works, O Lord!
    Your thoughts are very deep!
The dullard cannot know,
    the stupid cannot understand this:
though the wicked sprout like grass
    and all evildoers flourish,
they are doomed to destruction forever,
    but you, O Lord, are on high forever.
For your enemies, O Lord,
    for your enemies shall perish;
    all evildoers shall be scattered.

But you have exalted my horn like that of the wild ox;
    you have poured over me fresh oil.
My eyes have seen the downfall of my enemies;
    my ears have heard the doom of my evil assailants.

The righteous flourish like the palm tree,
    and grow like a cedar in Lebanon.
They are planted in the house of the Lord;
    they flourish in the courts of our God.
In old age they still produce fruit;
    they are always green and full of sap,
showing that the Lord is upright;
    he is my rock, and there is no unrighteousness in him.

— Psalm 92

ENDNOTES

1. Walter Brueggemann, "Covenant Spirituality," *New Conversations*, Winter 1977, p. 4.

2. Marjorie J. Thompson, *Soul Feast: An Invitation to the Christian Spiritual Life* (Louisville: Westminster John Knox Press, 1995), p. 6.

3. Evelyn Underhill, *The Ways of the Spirit* (Crossroad, N.Y.: Crossroad Publishing Company, 1990), p. 106.

4. Henri J. M. Nouwen, *With Open Hands* (Notre Dame, Ind.: Ave Maria Press, 1972), p. 120.

5. Henri J. M. Nouwen, *Out of Solitude* (Notre Dame, Ind.: Ave Maria Press, 1976), p. 27.

6. Macrina Wiederkehr, *A Tree Full of Angels* (New York: Harper & Row, Publishers, 1988), p. 27.

7. From the hymn, "Be Present at Our Table, Lord," (words by John Cennick), *The United Methodist Hymnal* (Nashville: The United Methodist Publishing House, 1989), #621.

8. From the hymn, "This Is the Day the Lord Hath Made" (words by Isaac Watts), *The United Methodist Hymnal* (Nashville: The United Methodist Publishing House, 1989), #658.

9. From the hymn, "The Day Is Past and Over" (trans. by John Mason Neale), *The United Methodist Hymnal* (Nashville: The United Methodist Publishing House, 1989), #683.

10. From the hymn, "Abide with Me" (words by Henry F. Lyte), *The United Methodist Hymnal* (Nashville: The United Methodist Publishing House, 1989), #700.

11. "A Covenant Prayer in the Wesleyan Tradition," *The United Methodist Hymnal* (Nashville: The United Methodist Publishing House, 1989), #607.